The
Battered
Child
in Canada

THE
BATTERED
CHILD
IN CANADA

Mary van Stolk

Revised Edition

McClelland and Stewart

The Canadian Publishers
McClelland and Stewart Limited
25 Hollinger Road, Toronto

For permission to reprint copyright material, grateful acknowledgement is made to: the Alpha Omega Honor Medical Society, for extracts from "Violence in Our Society" by B. F. Steele, in *Pharos*, vol. 33, 1970; *Family Circle*, for the extract from "An Interview with Dr. John Springer" by J. H. Pollack, in the October 1969 issue; Harvard University Press, for extracts from Violence Against Children by David G. Gil; *National Enquirer*, for extracts from the story "Average Americans Tell What Should Be Done to Parents Who Beat Their Children," copyright © 1970 by *National Enquirer*, Lantana, Florida; Schenkman Publishing Company, for extracts from *Radical Man* by C. Hampden-Turner; Drs. B. Steele, C. Pollock, and E. Davoren, for extracts from "Proceedings of the Conference on Patterns of Parental Behavior Leading to Physical Abuse of Children;" The University of Chicago Press, for extracts from *The Battered Child* edited by R. E. Helfer and C. H. Kempe, copyright © 1968 by The University of Chicago Press; James W. Prescott and *The Futurist* for excerpt from "Body Pleasure and the Origins of Violence," *The Futurist*, April 1975; Raymond I. Parnas and the *Wisconsin Law Review* for excerpt from "The Police Response to the Domestic Disturbance," *Wisconsin Law Review*, 1: 914-960, 1967. The charts at the chapter openings are adapted from J. T. Weston, "A Summary of Neglect and Traumatic Cases," in Helfer and Kempe, *The Battered Child*, copyright © 1968 by The University of Chicago Press.

Canadian Cataloguing in Publication Data

Van Stolk, Mary, 1931
    The battered child in Canada

ISBN 0-7710-8712-8

1. Child abuse—Canada. 2. Child welfare—
Canada. I. Title.

HV745.A6V3 1978   362.7'1   C78-001426-X

Manufactured in Canada by Webcom Limited

CONTENTS

To Cameron

ACKNOWLEDGEMENTS

The author wishes to acknowledge the special assistance of Karen Molgaard, who so ably researched and assisted in the editing and compilation of the material for this second edition. Her help in evaluating the diverse subject matter that had to be covered in a study of this kind was invaluable. Without her dedicated help and support I would have been unable to complete this study. And a continuing thank you to Paul Gregory for his assistance.

I would also like to thank the many interdisciplinary professionals across Canada who assisted in this study.

A special note of thanks to Dr. R. E. Helfer, Department of Human Development, Michigan State University, East Lansing, Michigan, who took time from his busy practice and the completion of his own manuscripts to review and suggest changes. His help was crucial in ensuring the accuracy of this study.

Also, to Dr. Christian Bay, Political Economy Department, The University of Toronto, who patiently reviewed the book and offered his greatly valued suggestions and criticisms.

Finally, to Jack McClelland for commissioning this book on the question of battered children in Canada, a problem that less courageous publishers might have hesitated to be involved in.

Over the six years since the publication of the first edition of this book, approximately six million children, in the United States and Canada, have been abused and/or neglected. This is 7 to 8 per cent of the children in these two countries. Considering that the most devastating effect upon the children who are abused and/or neglected, at least for those who survive without permanent physical damage, is to their personal development, this abuse becomes an enormous social and moral issue. This developmental damage most often leads to a permanent scarring which will take its toll in later years. If the result of abuse has adversely affected 7 to 8 per cent of children in the past six years, it will continue to climb, adding another one per cent to its toll each year. Society cannot afford the consequences.

The story is not all negative. These last half dozen years have seen significant progress in the area of early recognition and treatment. The work of thousands of motivated individuals is beginning to yield positive results, many of which are reviewed in this second edition. Even more encouraging is the movement toward prevention. The "state of the art" has finally reached the point where prevention programs can now begin. By the time the third edition appears, it will no longer be necessary to wait for the abuse or neglect to occur before helping in a positive manner. With continued efforts, the next generation should find considerably fewer breakdowns in the interactions between parents and their children.

The Battered Child in Canada has played, and will continue to play, an important role in the advancements in this field. Child abuse and neglect, in its present magnitude, is an unnecessary social illness. With the advent of preventive programs, young adults will receive the help, support, and training they need to interact positively with their children.

Ray E. Helfer, M.D., Professor
Department of Human Development
Michigan State University
East Lansing, Michigan, U.S.A.

"There are no lobbyists for children," writes Mary Van Stolk. And it is about time somebody tried to do something about it. Of all the cries for justice that should have a right to be heard, the cries of our battered children are the most anguished and yet the most muted. They are too seldom heard outside the walls of their not-so-sweet homes. The scars, the fright, the damages to body and spirit are visible, but individually and collectively most of us do our convenient best not to see them. And we tend to rationalize our cool tolerance of child abuse by the age-old reluctance to be our brothers' keepers.

In theory, if we think we have a democratic system of government, we may say that our brothers can look out for themselves. My work in political science has convinced me that while we have a good society, relatively speaking, for those of us who have good jobs or an independent income, we do not have a democracy; we don't have a society with equal rights or equal say for all, and we certainly don't have even the necessities of life for all. It is just not true that our brothers are in a position to look out for themselves, if our brothers happen to be poor, or sick, or uneducated, or old, or handicapped in any number of ways that nice people in suburbia may not be aware of.

Until we reach that utopian mirage, the Just Society, I don't see how we can remain human unless we in principle, in some sense at least, take it upon ourselves to be our less fortunate brothers' keepers—not to guide or preach but to help bolster their security and their freedom to choose how to live. You may agree or disagree with me so far; perhaps you feel that we should all be rugged individualists and sink or swim by ourselves. But even if you take this extreme view with respect to adults, I trust you will not expect the same of small children, or those children whose lives and health are being destroyed by malfunctioning parents. In short, I don't see how *any* human being who is exposed to the facts presented in this book can subsequently shrink from a sense of obligation to become his brother's children's keeper.

True, in practical terms it is not always easy to determine what is to be done, whenever we discover the awful truth, perhaps by looking into a terrified child's eyes. It is not always possible to translate an urgent sense of concern into effective action, especially in cases where we are a little less than a hundred per cent sure of the facts. But an urgent sense of concern is at least a beginning, and for someone who has reached that stage of responsibility as a human being there is much practical advice to be harvested in this book.

Mary Van Stolk carefully documents not only the likely extent of the problem of child battery, and the various legal angles and professional role limitations that explain and under-pin our continuing neglect of the problem; she also is very specific in her recommendations of remedies that are emi-nently feasible. Remedies in legislation, first of all, that will define the doctor's responsibilities more clearly, and more com-pellingly, and then remedies in the training of doctors, social workers, lawyers, and other professionals who under the pre-sent system often have no other convenient recourse but to wash their hands and dispatch the beaten child back home, to certain prospects of more torture. Too often, also, professionals have not learned what the sure symptoms of battery are, in the child or in the parent, or what avenues toward help may be open to the problem parent or parents.

Apart from giving us a wealth of practically useful advice on issues like these, Mary Van Stolk also urges all of us to take a good look at ourselves and try to reassess our own attitudes toward our children. Even if we in no sense are child batterers, don't we sometimes beat or abuse our children, without necess-ity or even good reasons? Or, even if we have never really struck a child, don't we tend to act and think as if our children were our personal property for us to enjoy, rather than sepa-rate human beings with developing personalities of their own, who need our protection to grow freely in response to their own inner needs?

Nevitt Sanford, the distinguished senior co-author of *The Authoritarian Personality* (New York: Harper, 1950), has said that it is a wonder that children don't become neurotic wrecks more often than they do, when you consider that they nearly all have to grow up as hostages in a mixed marriage: one man and one woman, members of two different species, almost, who somehow have to get along within the four walls of a home, and very often at the expense of their children. How many of us respect the integrity and dignity of our children, even at the teenage stage, to the extent that their deep wishes are taken as seriously as our own or those of our spouse?

More seriously—and this is one of the themes Mary Van Stolk has developed in her earlier work *Man and Woman* (Toronto: McClelland and Stewart, 1968)—is it not true that most North American parents will feel quite free to express anger and aggression directed at a child and yet feel quite put upon if the child responds in the same coin? In short, is it not part of our conventional wisdom to tolerate or even indulge in a lot of rudeness toward and abuse of children, with all-too-easy excuses to the effect that they need discipline, when in fact we could have used some self-discipline ourselves?

There is a world of difference, of course, between the many parents who lack respect for the dignity of their children, and the emotionally unstable parents who attack their children with sometimes crippling physical violence. There is a world of difference, too, between a sore throat and pneumonia, but it is helpful to realize that even a sore throat is something to be avoided if possible. Now, a sore throat doesn't *become* pneumonia, any more than the average moody and yet "strict" parent becomes a child batterer. But, and this is important, if sore throats are not a cause for concern then symptoms of developing pneumonia will be harder to detect, just as it is argued in this book that when it is common to push children around then the anguish of those children who are being crippled for life, or ultimately killed, is all the more likely to remain undetected until it is too late.

So let us become more sensitive to the needs of children, both others' and our own. Let us accept the notion that they, too, ought to have human rights, and even the right to a measure of respect and dignity, which their parents ought to recognize. This is a part of Mary Van Stolk's message, directed to her readers as parents or future parents, or as adults in their role of friends and neighbours or teachers of children. We can help, she believes, by becoming better tuned to their needs and rights. Not only can we help specific children by becoming pillars of emotional support and perhaps in nitty-gritty ways, too; but we can also by our sensitivity and good sense help improve the general atmosphere in our neighbourhoods, so that respect for the rights of children to be children, secure and free, becomes the "in" thing.

Yet the most urgent part of the author's message is addressed to us as citizens, in that she makes a strong case for the need for new legislation as well as new requirements of training in some of the professions. Judges called upon to make decisions that can mean life or death for an infant or child should disqualify themselves if they have had no training to acquaint them with the child-battering syndrome; such training should become incorporated in the legal curriculum for all future judges, as well as for police officers, social workers, and nurses. Can anyone disagree so far?

But Mary Van Stolk goes further and addresses some insistent questions to our mighty medical profession. Of all professionals, the medical doctor can do the most to help the battered child, or to seal its doom if he chooses. Medical examination can in most cases establish, with extremely low margins of error, whether child battery has taken place. And yet it is the rule rather than the exception that a careful examination is not made when it should be, or that the child is not being helped even when battery has been demonstrated. Why? Because there is no legal requirement that under pain of penalties compels reporting of child battery, and because the doctor may see a lot of inconvenience and time lost and even unpleasant consequences, to himself, if he does report.

The case for new legislation that will effectively require official reporting of all cases of child battery is argued very powerfully, in my judgment, in this book. But the reader must judge that for himself, or for herself. And draw his or her own conclusions regarding what we can do about this problem – as parents, as citizens, as professionals, and perhaps as human beings.

I hope this book will be read widely, and also by the many unhappy parents who are child batterers, always for reasons beyond their own control. Mary Van Stolk has a clear message to them, too: give up your lonely struggle with your own guilt and shame; you, too, love your children, so give them a chance; seek psychiatric advice before it might be too late.

This book will not only provoke thought and make many readers knowledgable about the plight of many children; it will, I believe, help save many lives.

Christian Bay, Ph.D., Professor
Political Economy Department
The University of Toronto

TYPICAL CASE PROFILE

AGE	three years
SEX	male
ASSAILANT	stepfather
RECENT EXTERNAL INJURIES	numerous bruises, face and trunk; large laceration, lip; numerous linear and loop abrasions, trunk
REMOTE EXTERNAL INJURIES	healing and healed linear and loop abrasions; healing burn, buttocks
FRACTURES	rib — recent
INTERNAL INJURIES	laceration — liver; contusions — lung, mesentery, and jejunum
CAUSE OF DEATH	laceration of liver with hemorrhage
PRESENTING STORY	"fell downstairs"
METHOD OF INJURY	placed on hot radiator to dry pants; beat with belt and switch; struck with hands
REASON FOR INJURY	"wet and messed pants"

CHAPTER 1
The Dimensions of Child Abuse

The first clues into what has become known as the Battered Child Syndrome were uncovered around the turn of the century by early researchers and radiologists.[1, 2] X-ray plates of small children and infants revealed fractures and other lesions which could not be explained by the medical histories of the children. However, more than forty years were to pass before studies were undertaken to determine the cause of these unexplained fractures.

In 1946, Dr. J. Caffey investigated the occurrence of multiple fractures in infants who also suffered from subdural hematoma.[3] Subdural hematoma is a blood clot enclosed within the skull which puts dangerous pressure on the brain. In the late thirties and early forties doctors accepted, almost to the exclusion of all other causes, the theory that subdural hematoma in infants and young children must be the result of trauma (injury).[4, 5] Caffey's study linked the mysterious fractures of the long bones in infants to the already accepted diagnosis of injury as the cause of subdural hematoma. He concluded that the multiple fractures in these infants were also traumatic in origin, rather than resulting from a rare exotic disease, as had been previously thought. This theory guided the investigations of subsequent researchers. More years of work and research were nevertheless required to confirm that these mysterious injuries were not due to unobserved or unreported household accidents, but were the result of abuse inflicted on children.

The difficulty of diagnosing the cause of these injuries is explained by the fact that abuse is most often inflicted on children too young to speak, making it impossible for them to explain how their injuries occurred. In 1962, Dr. C. H. Kempe, leading researcher and originator of the term "Battered Child Syndrome," stated: "If the child could only speak, the physician would be quickly led to the proper diagnosis of abuse. To the informed physician the bones tell a story the child is too young or too frightened to tell."[6]

The Battered Child Syndrome got its name from the child's injuries, which result from twisting, throwing, or knocking about. These injuries include bites, bruises, hematoma, and combinations of fractures of the arms, legs, skull or ribs. X-rays often reveal old fractures in various stages of healing, thus indicating that abuse has been repetitive.[7] This kind of abuse can be horribly severe and is fatal in two to four per cent of reported cases.

Gloria Jeliu, Director of the Protection Clinic at Ste. Justine's Hospital in Montreal, reports that just under five per cent of the children seen at the Clinic died from such maltreatment and thirty to forty per cent risked the after-effects of neurological disorders (paralysis, pseudo-retardation), physical disorders (disability, growth-retardation) or functional disorders (general backwardness in learning experience and knowledge, behaviour disorders, etc.).

In 1962, an editorial in the *Journal of the American Medical Association* suggested that when the full range becomes known, "it is likely that it [the Battered Child Syndrome] will be found to be a more frequent cause of death than such well-recognized and thoroughly studied diseases as leukemia, cystic fibrosis, and muscular dystrophy, and it may well rank with automobile accidents and the toxic **and infecti**ous encephalides **as causes of** acquired disturbances of the central nervous system."[8] In 1963 it was estimated that for every abused child who received medical attention, there must be at least a hundred who were not treated.[9]

On June 3, 1968, *Newsweek* reported that although complete figures were not available, at least sixty thousand children were willfully beaten, burned, smothered, and starved every year in the United States. In the United States more children under five die every year from injuries inflicted by a parent or guardian than from tuberculosis, whooping cough, polio, measles, diabetes, rheumatic fever, and appendicitis combined.[10]

Douglas J. Besharov, Director of the U.S. National Center on Child Abuse and Neglect, writing in the June 1976 issue of *Child Abuse and Neglect Reports*, states: "It is always hard to know the 'true incidence' of socially disapproved, and, indeed, criminal behavior which occurs behind closed doors in the privacy of the home. Nevertheless, research efforts in the last ten years, as well as [U.S.] State central register systems do allow us to make reasonable estimates. . . . We believe that it is reasonable to state that *if there were full reporting*, there would be approximately one million cases of child abuse *and neglect* reported annually."[11]

In Canada an accurate statistical picture is impossible to obtain (see Chapter Fifteen). However, public health authorities state that parents are among the greatest killers of Canadian infants. They also point out that the few statistics that are available reflect only a glimpse of actual incidences of abuse. The lack of statistics is due to a variety of factors. Parents make up believable stories; children are usually too young or too frightened to say what actually happened to them; and, strangely enough, most physicians fail to acknowledge the fact that parents could destroy their children, while some tend to keep silent for fear of possible legal consequences.[12]

The Minister of National Health and Welfare, commenting on the extent of the problem in his December 6th, 1975 presentation to the Parliamentary Standing Committee on Health, Welfare and Social Affairs studying child abuse and neglect in Canada stated:

> As of June 1975, there were approximately 68,000 children in the care of Child Welfare authorities in Canada as a result of neglect ranging from unintentional, circumstantial neglect to direct and willful neglect. Along

with the children removed from their homes, we know that as of the same date, Child Welfare authorities were working with over 42,000 families involving approximately 96,000 children, in order to protect children from neglect by attempting to correct or mitigate the potential or actual neglect situation in the home. We know that within the total number of neglected children and children in danger of being neglected, 1,085 were children found to be abused or battered in the year 1973-74. Child neglect then, is a very serious problem but the true extent of it is unknown. I have given you statistics on the numbers of neglected children known to Child Welfare authorities. The number of children in a state of neglect who have not come to the attention of any authority is the great unknown. I would also like to remind you that in describing neglect, I spoke of it in the legal context. Were we to expand neglect to include all children who are deprived of the right to develop to the maximum of their potential or, as it has been frequently expressed, allowed to thrive, we might well be describing a much larger number of children in our society.[13]

At the time of the Minister's presentation, few provinces in Canada maintained or had available statistics on child abuse. Yet, according to Helfer and Kempe, the same year, 1975, saw one per cent of American children reported as abused, with an unknown number of unreported cases doubtless swelling the actual percentage.[14] Such a statistic could well reflect the situation for Canada in that year.

Research in Canada on the question of abused children discloses a gross unawareness of the child abuse syndrome on the part of pediatricians and general practitioners. This fact is reflected throughout the literature on child abuse, both in the United States and Canada, where, again and again, we find researchers in this area urging interdisciplinary colleagues to acquaint themselves with the child abuse syndrome and to recognize the frequent occurrence and seriousness of child abuse cases.[15-19]

Although it is necessary to differentiate between child battering, other physical abuse, child neglect, and emotional abuse, all can result in severe damage to the child and are classified as child abuse. Neglect can involve failure to nourish, either physically and/or emotionally, to provide sanitary living conditions, to supervise adequately, to clothe, or to obtain medical aid for one's children.[20] Neglect may occur because the parents or other caretakers hate the child or are ignorant, apathetic, or depressed. They may be in a poor state of health, in financial difficulties, or simply unaware of what is necessary to sustain a child. Some parents both batter and neglect, and this abuse can be carried to a point where the child may die.

Failure to thrive is a part of the physical abuse of children.

Kempe states that twenty per cent of failure to thrive cases studies "are due to deficiency in mothering, either not enough food, or emotional neglect, or aversion. It is a serious, and often missed, form of the child abuse syndrome."[21] The seriousness of failure to thrive is illustrated by recent studies which found that insufficient amounts of protein during the first five months of life results in permanent retardation.[22] Another study found that infants who were successfully treated for failure to thrive and returned to the home were subsequently battered by their parents.[23]

Child battering exists when physical injuries are inflicted on a child by the child's caretaker. The caretaker injuring the child is usually a parent, but may be another relative, such as older brother or sister, a baby-sitter, a teacher, or anyone else who is temporarily taking care of the child.

A summary of the kinds of abuse which have been inflicted on children makes clear the distinction between abuse and neglect. Children have been punched, kicked, pinched, bitten, scratched, and flung against hard objects. They have been beaten with whips, cooking utensils, electric cords, and belts; hit by sticks, tree branches, heavy books, building materials, garden tools, furniture, coat hangers, and high-heeled shoes. They have been stabbed, burned, locked for days in closets, put out of the house in their night clothes in zero weather, chained to bed posts, and plunged into cold rivers, as well as placed in scalding baths. Boiling water and coffee are the most common causes of scalds. Infants are fed boiling milk. Contact burns are inflicted on children by placing them on hot stoves or surface heating units. Children are thrown on the grates of floor furnaces and burned by cigarettes; cremation was actually attempted on one infant.[24, 25] Child battering is the extreme end of a spectrum of physical abuse of children occuring in our society.

The actual attacks on an infant or child* are usually made by one parent, with the other permitting it to occur. This is true even when the child is in the womb. While researching abused and battered children, I became aware that children were being beaten within the womb.[26] Many sources of infor-

*The vast majority of deaths among battered children occur in youngsters under the age of four. However, we have adopted the definition of a child as anyone who is under sixteen years of age. This is in accordance with the Child Welfare Acts of most of the provinces of Canada.

mation support the notion that physical violence and pregnancy are more highly associated than is commonly realized. For instance, many newspaper accounts of intrafamilial violence and homicide note that the wife/victim was pregnant at the time of the attack. Some wives who were hit when pregnant reported that the beating was followed by a miscarriage. Others told of handicapped children born after beatings. As one mother confided to researcher Richard J. Gelles: "Oh yea, he hit me when I was pregnant. It was weird. Usually he hit me in the face with his fist, but when I was pregnant he used to hit me in the belly. It was weird."[27]

Whether on a conscious or subconscious level, violence towards a pregnant wife may be a form of prenatal child abuse or filicide. Many researchers believe it may be a husband's attempt to terminate pregnancy and relieve him of the impending stress of yet another child.

Gelles believes that for many families, violence which brings about a miscarriage is a more acceptable way of terminating an unwanted pregnancy than is abortion. On the one hand, we know that there is still considerable controversy over the moral and legal aspects of abortion. "On the other hand, research on violence indicates violence is typical of family life. Consequently, violence which terminates a pregnancy may be more acceptable socially, morally, and even legally than is an abortion."[28]

Some studies indicate that more women attack children, but only because they are more often the caretakers. Where the mothers work and the fathers are in charge of children, the reverse is true.[29] Originally it was believed that mothers were the major batterers of children. However, since 1961, when Kempe first started studying child abuse, new studies reveal that, overall, men batter and abuse more frequently than women. Cyril Greenland, in his 1973 study on *Child Abuse in Ontario*, also found that more men than women were reported and verified as having abused their children.[30]

There has been a bias towards the concept of women as the major abusers of children. Child abuse literature consistently stressed battering women, when in fact even the early records showed an almost fifty-fifty split between male and female child abusers.[31, 32]

Recently, in testimony prepared for a U.S. House Science Subcommittee hearing on household violence, Besharov said that new research showed a relationship, perhaps a chain reaction, between spouse-beating and child abuse in some violent families. An investigation of child abuse cases in some twenty-five states found that in twenty per cent of the cases a spouse also was beaten, but not necessarily at the same time. One treatment project concluded that in many cases of family violence the victim is whatever family member happened to be available. "It is now apparent from the research ... that the injury of spouses (predominantly women) and the injury of children are somewhat overlapping syndromes."

Besharov said the research shows that while males are the abusers in only forty per cent of all officially reported child abuse and neglect cases, males are the perpetrators of seventy per cent of the child abuse cases that also involved an incidence of spouse abuse. "In these cases it appears that the violence of the male is directed at all members of the family." The research also indicates that in the other thirty per cent of officially reported cases in the same household in which the man is assaulting the mother, the mother is assaulting the child. Besharov noted that an analysis of research by the American Humane Association documents the relationship of spouse-beating and child abuse.[33]

The average age of the abusing mother is twenty-six; of the father approximately thirty. Thus there is no support for the commonly held belief that child abuse is the result of teenage marriage. The literature stresses that child abusers come from all walks of life and all kinds of backgrounds.[34] Child abuse occurs among families living in small towns, metropolitan areas and rural communities; and their housing varies from substandard hovels to high-class suburban homes. It is interesting to note that their houses are usually well kept. The educational achievements of child abusers range from partial grade school education all the way to post-doctoral degrees. The general level of intelligence, as measured in I.Q. tests, runs anywhere from the low seventies to superior ratings of 130 or more. Periods of unemployment depend upon the education and background of the abuser, and even the marital situations of child abusers do not seem significantly different from others in their own socio-economic group.[35]

Information on religious, racial, and ethnic backgrounds is limited. However, what information is available suggests that there is a link between child abuse and racial, religious, and ethnic backgrounds.[36] Among those people who are actively involved in their religion there is a greater than average adherence to a very strong, rigid, authoritative, fundamentalist type of belief.[37] Overall, however, *the battering of children is something that occurs throughout the population*.[38]

A significant new finding is that alcoholism is a major problem related to child abuse.[39] It is apparent from British reports that alcohol does play a significant role in the battered wife-child syndrome, whether among the rich or the poor.[40] American studies of interpersonal violence report a high association between alcohol and violence. One important feature of these findings was that alcohol-related violence is almost exclusively male violence.[41]

Jerry Cooper, Chief of Psychiatry at York Finch General Hospital in Toronto, in his work with abusing families, noted that: "It was quite rare to see alcohol as part of the mother's problems. However, for a majority of the women, alcohol had been a major problem, either in their own upbringing when they had experienced an alcoholic parent, or later when they had been married to an alcoholic. In some cases drugs were involved, particularly amphetamines."[42]

Factors which have been associated with child abuse and neglect include: a parental history of abuse or neglect as a child; stressful life circumstances including poverty, chronic illness, and unemployment; social isolation and associated lack of support; youth and associated inexperience; unwanted pregnancy, and absence of one parent. Many families in which one or both parents are alcoholics experience one or more of these situational factors. Although little is known about the incidence of abuse or neglect in the childhoods of alcoholics, Joseph Mayer and Rebecca Black of the Washingtonian Center for Addictions, believe that alcoholism as a chronic illness frequently leads to unemployment and poverty. Rejection of the alcoholic by society and the feelings of shame experienced by other family members contribute to social isolation and marital difficulties often disrupt these marriages, leaving a single parent family or leading to unwanted pregnancies.

Personality characteristics associated with the occurrence of child abuse and neglect include: low frustration tolerance, low self-esteem, impulsivity, dependency, immaturity, retardation, psychosis, severe depression, role reversal, difficulty in experi-

8

encing pleasure, and misperception and lack of understanding of the needs and abilities of infants and children. Impulsivity, dependency, and depression are characteristics often attributed to alcoholics. Low self-esteem is also characteristic of alcoholics, sometimes viewed as a reason for alcoholism and sometimes as a consequence of it. As previously mentioned, the difficulty in functioning experienced by the alcoholic frequently results in role reversals within the family, reversals in which children are expected to function as adults, while the alcoholic requires care, is not expected to function, and becomes the focus of attention. In addition, the spouse of the alcoholic may turn to the child, in lieu of the mate, for support and aid. Finally, lack of time and energy associated with the management of a chronic, disabling disease such as alcoholism may result in lack of attention to and understanding of the needs and abilities of infants and children.

Although not all alcoholics seriously abuse or neglect their children, the majority have difficulties in child-rearing. Many of the alcoholics are children of alcoholic parents themselves. In addition, male alcoholics report use of physical discipline by their parents. These fathers, in turn, report having high expectations of their own children and using physical punishment in disciplining their children, although they feel that they do not discipline as harshly as their parents did. For example, they may use their hands or cloth belts instead of a leather strap.[43]

Val MacMurray, Associate Professor with the Division of Community Health Science, University of Calgary, in his 1977 study of the Alberta provincial records covering 1974-76 inclusive, notes that while there is no firm statistical data because of the incompleteness of provincial records, a definite link between alcohol and child abuse exists, particularly in the neglect of children. MacMurray believes that when more complete records are available for research, the relationship between alcohol, abuse, and neglect will be an important factor.[44]*

Another form of child abuse is, of course, the damage to the unborn child through alcohol consumption during pregnancy. As Dr. Ann P. Streisguth concludes in *Alcoholism Problems in Women and Children:* "Based on the evidence ... we feel that

---

MacMurray found that the provincial registry files were very poorly kept, inconsistent, and not designed to facilitate research.

mental impairment is probably the most disabling aspect in children who do have the fetal alcohol syndrome."[45] The degree of mental retardation in children showing the fetal alcohol syndrome appears directly related to the gross physical deformities present in a given patient.[46]

Ruth and Henry Kempe point out that: "Alcoholic and drug addicted parents are minimally capable of caring for children since their intoxication makes them unsafe unless they are in a controlled, safe environment. Treatment may be very long and difficult, and significant improvement must occur before these parents are able to care for a child on their own. Many in this group will never be able to parent adequately, for the urgency of the child's own developmental timetable will preclude such a delay."[47]

While it is true that some parents who are unemployed and in financial straits, who live in poor housing units, have shattered marriages, or alcoholic difficulties, abuse their children, it does not follow that parents who are abstemious, devout, intelligent, or stably married and financially solvent do not attack their children. These are facts well-recognized by the people who work in the area of child abuse. But these facts must be stressed again and again because a large segment of our population, including many doctors, are still inclined to believe that child abuse occurs only among people of a low socio-economic status. This simply is not true.[48]

People who abuse their children have the same kinds of general mental disorders evidenced by the general population. They can be hysterical or obsessive-compulsive; they can be schizoid personalities or they can have character neuroses; they can experience anxiety states or depression and so forth, but it has not yet been possible for researchers to make a single or simple diagnosis of most abusers.[49]

Approximately 10 to 15 per cent of parents seen have psychiatric diagnoses that make their potential for treatment very poor. These diagnoses include parents who are psychotic, particularly those who appear as paranoid schizophrenic or schizophrenic patients with a delusional system that involves the child as part of the delusional system.[50]

The Kempes, along with other major researchers, find that: "A final group which has responded very poorly to treatment is a comparatively small group of parents who are 'fanatic' – those parents who have a highly fixed set of ideas that are ordinarily considered eccentric and that probably represent obsessional ideas in psychiatric terms. They are frequently related to a fundamentalist religion or an unusual philosophy of life. They may sometimes be extremely moralistic, very successful and very well respected people – 'pillars of society' – making the diagnosis very difficult. When their ideas include unusual exploitation of children, and establish deviant standards of behavior plus unusual and cruel punishments, this becomes a very dangerous environment for children. Their rigidity is a well established ideational system and they are very resistant to treatment."[51]

However, to state that all child abusers are immature or impulse-ridden, dependent or sadomasochistic, egocentric or narcissistic or demanding, is simply not correct. These terms can be applied to people in general, but they give little information about the psychological make-up of these individuals. People may be grossly immature, but that does not mean they will batter their children.[52]

The phenomenon of child battering takes place within a much larger field of child abuse, of which it forms, with emotional abuse, one of the most serious areas as well as one of the most difficult to expose. Child battering is part of the overall problem of child abuse. In its scope, child abuse includes much more than the tragedy of the battered child.

David G. Gil of Brandeis University gives a definition of child abuse in his book *Violence Against Children:*

> Physical abuse of children is the intentional, nonaccidental use of physical force, or intentional, nonaccidental acts of omission, on the part of a parent or other caretaker interacting with a child in his care, aimed at hurting, injuring, or destroying that child.[53]

Gil's definition of child abuse, which includes a much wider range of transactions than is included in the definition of child battering, was used as the criterion for a nation-wide study of child abuse in the United States. Gil reported that the overall phenomenon of the physical abuse of children is multi-dimensional. It results from the stress of social and economic factors as well as from factors stemming from emotional problems.[54]

Gil states that:

> Poverty ... appears to be related to the phenomenon of physical abuse of children in at least four ways. First, the cultural approval of the use of physical force in child-rearing tends to be stronger among the socio-economically deprived strata of society than among the middle class. Secondly, there seems to be less inhibition to express and discharge ag-

gressive and violent feelings and impulses toward other persons among members of socio-economically deprived strata than among the middle class. Thirdly, environmental stress and strain are considerably more serious for persons living in poverty than for those enjoying affluence. Finally, the poor have fewer opportunities than the nonpoor for escaping occasionally from child-rearing responsibilities.[55]

Gil's studies emphasize that the overall question of abuse is more widespread than the specific question of child battering and is symptomatic of a much larger and more serious cultural crisis.[56]

Definitions of neglect have focused on acts of omission by a parent or caretaker in providing such things as food, clothing, medical attention, supervision, education, and other things that society considers vital to a child's care. The definition offered by Polansky, Hally, and Polansky is the most comprehensive: "Child neglect may be defined as a condition in which a caretaker responsible for the child either deliberately or by extraordinary inattention permits suffering and/or fails to provide one or more of the ingredients generally deemed essential for developing a person's physical, intellectual and emotional capacities."[57]

Giovannoni and Becerra, in their 1977 study, found that four groups of professionals are involved in the management of child abuse and neglect cases – lawyers, doctors, social workers, and police – and that in part the issue of definitional differences reflects the lack of consensus among these professionals. Evidence of such definitional disagreement was indicated by the failure of some to define as abusive or neglectful individual cases that others put in this category.[58]

AGE	ten months
SEX	female
ASSAILANT	foster mother
RECENT EXTERNAL INJURIES	numerous bruises of face, laceration of lip
REMOTE EXTERNAL INJURIES	healing linear abrasions, buttocks and lower extremities
FRACTURES	humerus — healing; skull — recent
INTERNAL INJURIES	contusions, brain; subdural hemorrhage
CAUSE OF DEATH	subdural hemorrhage
PRESENTING STORY	"baby fell from table"
METHOD OF INJURY	beaten with hand, cord, and wooden ruler
REASON FOR INJURY	"excessive crying after fracture of humerus when first handled"

CHAPTER 2
Why Parents Batter Their Children

A significant number of people in our culture either know of someone who has been physically abused, as distinct from battered, or have themselves been abused to some degree or another.[1] Since varying degrees of physical abuse of children are so common as to be accepted by most people, it appears to many as something which is impossible to prevent. The specific nature of child battering must be examined, therefore, in order clearly to define it within the overall problem of child abuse. It is important to repeat that there are varying degrees of child abuse within which the Battered Child Syndrome is the extreme case of non-accidental injury to the child, ranging from the minimal to severe paralysis, blinding, maiming, or death. Many people have experienced a cuff on the ear, a harsh slap across the face, or a hard spanking. However, these forms of child abuse do not constitute the Battered Child Syndrome.

It is in the attitude of the parents towards the child that the overall theme of battering emerges. Most battered children are abused consistently from infancy.[2] Dr. Brandt Steele observes that after four years of studying the parents of abused children,

> the common denominator of our patients has been an adherence to a pattern of child rearing characterized by demand for premature high performance and satisfaction of parental needs. Accompanying this is complete disregard for what the infant might need and for his performance possibilities.
>
> Specifically, these parents – and I include anyone taking care of children – do not perceive the infant as an infant, but as an organized human being capable of sensing the parent's needs and meeting them. This phenomenon exists independently of variables such as socio-economic station, psychiatric diagnosis, age, sex, or relationship of the caretaker to the mistreated child.
>
> In all our patients who have attacked children, we have seen a breakdown in *ability to mother*. There is no great difference between men or women in this breakdown. By "mothering" we don't mean the superficial techniques of care, but the deep, sensitive, intuitive awareness of, and response to, the infant's condition and needs, as well as consideration of the infant's capacity to perform according to his age.[3]

Battering parents function quite normally in everyday circumstances. It is only in the interaction between themselves and their children that the problem arises.

To battering parents, the child is seen as something more than a child who needs care. Amazingly these parents regard children – even small infants – as capable of adult responses and comprehension. It is this belief that their children are capable of perceiving as adults which allows the peculiar emotional justification of their demands. In times of stress these parents often expect their children to understand the tremendous needs of the parents for love and approval.[4] They feel their children have the ability, through their adult understanding, to fulfil these needs. The child is expected to do this by being good and loving toward the parents and, of course, by obeying.

Also, many battering parents have been found to have unusually strong wishes to be "good" parents, although they are insecure about their parental abilities.[5] The child's behaviour is used to verify these abilities. If the child behaves as a "good" child, then the parent feels worthwhile. To the battering parent the child becomes a major source of fulfilment for the parent's own emotional needs. So long as the child is able to meet the parent's needs, the relationship runs smoothly. If, however, the child fails to satisfy these needs, by misbehaving or disobeying, or by sheer inability to comprehend, the parent's role as a "good" parent is threatened. If relief from the threatening situation is not available, a battering incident may very well occur.

The battering parent cannot identify with the child as a human being with limited capabilities, control and comprehension. The child is punished in order to force it to meet the parent's needs and demands. If the child continues to "disobey," these parents believe they have every right to be more and more punitive.

> Two little boys, age five months and sixteen months, were brought into the Colorado General Hospital with multiple bruises, lacerations, and fractures. Their father, Henry J., who had injured them, told us: "Children have to be taught respect for authority and be taught obedience. I would rather have my children grow up afraid of me and respecting me than loving me and spoiled." He had injured the children during routine disciplinary punishment intended to teach them good behaviour.[6]
>
> Henry J., in speaking of his sixteen-month-old son, Johnny, said, "He knows what I mean and understands it when I say 'come here.' If he doesn't come immediately, I go and give him a gentle tug on the ear to remind him of what he is supposed to do." In the hospital it was found that Johnny's ear was lacerated and partially torn away from his head.[7]

The clue to understanding the acts of such a parent is that the parent feels justified; he feels righteous; he feels not only that he is doing the right thing, but that there is a necessity for him to have done what he did. Within the context of his belief it would have been wrong to have allowed the transgressions of the child to go unpunished.

> A mother, Holly T., whose five-month-old baby suffered a fractured skull and a fractured pelvis, told us how children have to be taught to be obedient, to respond to parental demands, and to take care of themselves and not expect too much from their parents. She said that her little baby, age five and a half months, was lazy and stubborn, and therefore needed discipline.[8]

To quote Drs. Brandt Steele and Carl Pollock:

> Following the attack, some parents may maintain a strict, righteous attitude, express no sense of guilt about the aggression, insist they have done nothing wrong, and are very resentful toward anyone who tries to interfere with their affairs. On the other hand, some parents are filled with remorse, weep, and quickly seek medical help if the child has been seriously hurt.
>
> It has not been possible in all patients to obtain a clear story of what they actually did to the child at the time a serious injury ocurred, even though abuse is admitted. They insist they did nothing differently than usual. In some cases this may be a defensive forgetting. In others it is probably a true statement. They have been hitting or yanking the child routinely and are not aware of the extra force used at the time of fracture.[9]

Why does a parent believe that it was right and proper to

have burned a child for some misbehaviour? How is it that a parent could feel righteous for having broken the arm or leg of a child because it disobeyed? How is it possible that a parent could feel that he or she had done the best thing for the child or the infant, by flinging it across the room to make it stop crying? How is it that otherwise rational people can maintain this feeling of righteousness about the kind of punishment which they inflict upon children?

The answers, in part, lie in the fact that the parents have been told, and believe, that it is absolutely essential to make the child "behave."[10] Further, they sincerely believe that terrible things will happen to the child when he grows up if he does not learn to obey authority.

> Henry J. recalls that his father frequently beat him and his brothers with straps, sticks and boards, and remembers his father often saying, "I'm going to teach you boys to respect authority. I don't want you to grow up to be juvenile delinquents." Holly told us that her mother tells her, "You better teach those kids to behave better. Sammy ought to have his butt blistered every time he turns around."[11]

The parent is supported in this belief by the society.[12] Almost every aspect of the culture promotes the idea that unquestioning obedience must be demanded, and given, or society will crumble. This is the way the schools, the churches, the armies, and the government are structured. This is the way we are taught to behave in our society.*

Though our culture supports the idea of punitive discipline, the primary question still remains: why is it that a parent, hearing the screams of agony from his child, does not respond? Why does he not stop and comfort the child? He does not respond to the screams from his child because no one responded to his screams when he was a child. This is the strongest and indeed the key factor in the whole Battered Child Syndrome. In almost every instance the parents of battered children were themselves either physically or emotionally abused as children by their own parents.[18-21]

The parent does not *feel* because he was not taught to *feel*. That is why he does not respond to the screams of his child.

---

*This is a factor in our society which has been increasingly described by many and various disciplines, and is well presented in such writings as: Jules Henry, Culture Against Man; Hannah Arendt, On Violence; Christian Bay, The Structure of Freedom; George Leonard, Education and Ecstasy; and Charles Hampden-Turner, Radical Man. [13-17]

He never learned to empathize with other human beings. He never learned to be a good parent.

The ability to be a good mother or father is learned.[22] Love and hate are not a part of our instincts; feelings and responses are taught in much the same way as languages are taught. Society can teach the child to speak any language that it can invent. It can also teach the child to act out any kind of emotional language. It can teach the child to despise or love himself. It can teach him to respect or to be disrespectful of himself and others; to be a loving, kind, warm human being or a disrespectful, rude, unkind, unloving one. *Parents teach all this by example and their treatment of the child from infancy onwards.* "Abuse, like other behaviour, becomes habitual. Children learn from the behaviour they witness and experience. They internalize conceptions of themselves communicated to them by others."[23]

Parents can be without feeling for their children because, as children, they were dealt with in such a way as to make it quite clear that no one was prepared to listen or respond to their needs. The constant example that they experienced as children was the urgent necessity to obey instantly all parental commands. They learned that something terrible happened if parental authority was not immediately obeyed. It follows that when the battered child grows up to be a parent and a child batterer, that person is quite simply carrying out the training for parenthood that he or she received as a child. The key factor, therefore, in the making of human beings who are incapable of battering their children, is the training and response to human beings that they experience when they are growing up. We are good parents insofar as we train our children by example to be good parents.

With this information it is possible to begin looking into the feelings, or if you like the absence of feelings, in the personality of abusing parents. Battering results from no metaphysical inborn tendency towards mischief or evil. It is a question of cause and effect. It is now possible to realize that this adult can be quite charming, have a gay sense of humour, be talented and creative, well-dressed, enjoy and love music, be politically astute, well-read, have good taste, be a good business person, save money, be neat in his personal habits, keep himself and his children clean and well-dressed, be in favour of all the right causes, be appalled by all the wickedness that goes on in the world, be concerned and alert as a citizen, and still, as a battered child grownup, batter children.

This person may have memories of a miserable childhood and realize that his or her parents were terribly harsh. Or perhaps he or she denies that the parents were harsh, and justifies the abuse that was received by rationalizing in the following way: "My parents were right to be tough with me. I guess I was a little bit of a heller. I needed to be taken in tow. I am very grateful to them for straightening me out."

This person has wants and desires, wants to fall in love with the right man or woman, wants to live in pleasant surroundings, wants to have a good job or be married to someone who has a good job, and wants to have the good life in general. With these feelings and intent, the person who was battered as a child meets another individual, falls in love and marries. If circumstances are right and their first child is easy, doesn't have colic and responds well, that is, if this child is lucky enough not to cause the parents any difficulty or trouble, then chances are that everything may go reasonably well.[24] The child eats when it is supposed to eat, sleeps when it is supposed to sleep, laughs when it is supposed to laugh and, in general, fulfils the parental expectations. And so it builds a relationship with its parents. By chance this child never calls forth the parent's underlying rage, which is ready to flash out at anything that doesn't obey and respond.

Now, suppose that these parents have a second child. This child, unlike the first, is difficult right from the beginning. The baby is colicky and nothing seems to please it.[25] The parents can't figure out what is wrong and begin to have an uneasy feeling. The child is thought to be willful and disobedient. The parents begin to suspect that there is something not quite right about this child.[26] They have mixed feelings of concern, anger, and dislike towards the child, as well as confusion about their role as parents. They also are concerned that the child may get spoiled from being picked up too frequently, or they may feel that it is already spoiled.

Let us suppose that it is the mother who is the battered child grownup. The child cries a lot and the mother does not know what to do or how to seek help. The crying makes the mother feel angry and desperate.[27] She reacts by being rough, by shaking and sometimes striking the infant to make it stop crying.

The mother is incapable of understanding the child's needs. When it cries, her first response is that it must be hungry and so she *insists* that it eat. Every child will eat as much as it needs to eat, and past that it will spit out the food or even vomit it up. Every adult knows the point of limit where they themselves do not want any more food. But where an adult can in fact say no, an infant cannot. The way an infant says no more, is by moving its head aside to try to avoid the spoon or nipple, or by pushing the food out of its mouth with its tongue, and eventually by thrashing about and crying and making it quite clear that it is an unpleasant experience to have to eat any more.

However, to a mother who has been battered herself as a child, or has been raised by very unloving, punitive parents, refusing food constitutes a threat to her authority. She has interpreted the child's crying as a need for food. She rigidly clings to this view, not only because she has incorrectly decided how much food the child should eat, but because a child who eats gives her a feeling of satisfaction and proves that she is a good mother. When the child does not eat, this not only threatens her authority but makes her insecure. A very important facet of the Battered Child Syndrome is the parent's feeling that the child should provide satisfaction to the parents by being "good," so that the parents can feel they are "good" parents.[28] The child must provide love at all times to the parents in the form of performance and obedience in order to satisfy their feelings of insecurity.

Let us say that the child is now about six months old. The mother not only forces food upon it, but also expects it to be able to sit still and eat without ever making a mess. When it fails to do this, it is punished. With every meal there is conflict between the mother and the child. After every meal the mother is distraught and upset. The mother finds the child difficult and feels righteously aggravated and cross.[29]

The child will not eat. The mother's attitude becomes more rigid and fixed. "You must eat this; you will eat this; you will eat this if we have to sit here all day until you do eat," and the child is slapped and struck to make it obey. Here then begins one of the major areas of conflict and abuse – the question of food and who is going to eat what, and when, and how much.[30]

Because of the experiences with food, the mother believes

that for some strange reason of its own this willful child does not want to obey. However, the mother "knows" it is her job to force this child to eat and that it must obey. Further, this woman has the experience of her "good" first child to fall back on. She says to herself and her husband, "Our first child never gave us a bit of trouble; our first child was a normal, happy baby." Implicit in that statement is: "This child gives us a lot of trouble and that must mean it isn't quite normal. We know what normal babies do – they eat well, respond nicely, coo at us and are never difficult. This child doesn't do that. He is different [i.e. bad]."

Since the mother is already poorly disposed towards this child, her feeling is one of anxiety about whether the child will be difficult to toilet train. At a very early age the child must live up to the rigid standards for toilet training which the mother sets.[31] In toilet training no child can perform on schedule. When he cannot perform, or has an accident, he is seen as having deliberately thwarted the mother's attempts to see that he did the right thing, and is punished accordingly.

The mother and the child are in conflict, and the lines of battle are drawn. The mother believes that her job is to win. She must fight this child and curb it, make it obey and force it to do what is right and proper. The child must do everything that she tells it to do immediately on command. If the child could meet these demands, this would prove to her that she is a "good" mother.

Crying too is viewed by the mother as an insult to her authority. She feels that she is doing the right thing for the child. She is driven to strike the child by what she feels is the child's miserable behaviour. The child should not cry. The mother, out of a confused mixture of guilt, self-righteousness and fury, strikes the child again, perhaps even more severely than the first time. At this point anything can happen. The child may be picked up and shaken and, if it is still screaming and struggling violently, it may be flung across the room.

These are the ingredients of child battering; they can occur either sporadically or consistently. As a result of this sort of treatment, an arm or leg may be broken, ribs may be fractured, internal organs injured; there may be permanent brain damage, or the child may die. But perhaps the child is lucky; perhaps no ribs or arms are broken. Somehow the child escapes from this incident and the others that follow, without

20

any major injuries. Nevertheless a consistent pattern of abuse has been enacted upon it, with the concomitant emotional battering and the deprivation of love, empathy and mothering which are so necessary to the making of human beings. What has also taken place is a transfer of information, attitude and action from one generation to another. The parent is passing on to the child, and to the other children in the family, a distinct method of child rearing. The parent is training her children in a manner *similar* to the training she received from her parents.[32]

By the manner in which they deal with the child, parents teach what it is like to be a parent: how to look, how to talk and how to respond to infants and to children. What the child sees is what the parent saw as a child. The battering parent is giving out what she saw her own parents do, in one degree or another, when she withdrew from food or struggled against her parents. This battered child grownup experienced as a child the strong emotional reaction of parents when a situation did not go their way.

The response of these adults is usually consistent with the pattern of their own upbringing. This woman is doing what she was taught to do when she was a child. So far as she is concerned, no other response would be appropriate. She sees no real alternative to her actions during the time of the incident. After the situation has passed she may be very sorry and regret the incident, as battering parents sometimes do. However, this regret will be of no assistance to her on the next occasion because her regret is based on an intellectual summation of what has taken place, while the actual battering of the child was based on an emotionally-learned process. The two are quite separate.

Dr. Steele observes that

> the parents are insensitive to the ebb and flow of the infant's needs. They are concentrating more on the needs they themselves have. This is role reversal in which parents act like a needy child and expect their child to take over the role of a satisfying parent.
>
> This is a repetition of the parents' own childhood situation. They feel unloved, unlistened to, uncared for, and deeply worthless. We don't mean they didn't receive attention from their parents and families. On the contrary, they were often the focus of extreme concern which took the form of demand and attack rather than anything approximating kindness and sympathy. Their own sense of worth came when they were able to meet the exorbitant parental demands described, but this was rare and transient. Although this situation occurs at all levels of society, the type of performance demanded may be socio-economically determined.

21

The intensity of our patients' super-ego is striking. They are quite punitive and rigid. This shows up in psychological tests as well as in clinical data we obtain from them...

When the child fails to perform in a way to make the parent feel good, the child becomes an evil environment, so to speak. Anger, resentment, and fury are aroused in the parent who then identifies the child with his own critical parent.

We have found that even though abusers feel their own parents were demanding and belittling of them, rarely have they faced their parents with this in reality.

As a rule, the child is not attacked on this identification basis alone. The abuser usually does not hit the child until he can rework the situation to see the child as his own bad, needy, crying self. Then the super-ego can approve the attack and punishment, because in this super-ego structure the parent has a right to attack a no-good infant. Repeatedly we hear parents say that hitting their baby was like hitting themselves.

Attacking parents look to other people for mothering besides their own mothers. Women look to husbands particularly, husbands look to wives. But if the mothering function fails in the environment, the parent quickly takes it out on the baby.[33]

Extending Steele's work on parental misfunction, James W. Prescott, a developmental neuropsychologist and a health scientist administrator with the National Institute of Child Health and Human Development, U.S. National Institutes of Health, writes:

the deprivation of physical sensory pleasure is the principal root cause of violence. Laboratory experiments with animals show that pleasure and violence have a reciprocal relationship, that is, *the presence of one inhibits the other*. A raging, violent animal will abruptly calm down when electrodes stimulate the pleasure centers of its brain. Likewise, stimulating the violence centers in the brain can terminate the animal's sensual pleasure and peaceful behavior. When the brain's pleasure circuits are "on", the violence circuits are "off," and vice-versa. Among human beings, a pleasure-prone personality rarely displays violence or aggressive behaviors, and a violent personality has little ability to tolerate, experience, or enjoy sensuously pleasing activities. As either violence or pleasure goes up, the other goes down.

The reciprocal relationship of pleasure and violence is highly significant, because certain sensory experiences during the formative periods of development will create a neuropsychological predisposition for either violence-seeking or pleasure-seeking behaviors later in life.

Prescott found that "the deprivation of body touch, contact, and movement are the basic causes of a number of emotional disturbances that include depressive and autistic behaviors, hyperactivity, sexual aberration, drug abuse, violence, and aggression." According to Prescott,

These insights were derived chiefly from the controlled laboratory studies of Harry F. and Margaret K. Harlow at the University of Wisconsin. The Harlows and their students separated infant monkeys from their mothers at birth. The monkeys were raised in single cages in an animal colony room, where they could develop social relationships with the other animals through seeing, hearing, and smelling, but not through touching or movement. These and other studies indicate that it is the deprivation of body contact and body movement – not deprivation of the other senses – that produces the wide variety of abnormal emotional behaviors in these isolation-reared animals. It is well known that human infants and children who are hospitalized or institutionalized for extended periods with little physical touching and holding develop almost identical abnormal behaviors, such as rocking and head banging.

Although the pathological violence observed in isolation-reared monkeys is well documented, the linking of early somatosensory deprivation with physical violence in humans is less well established. Numerous studies of juvenile delinquents and adult criminals have shown a family background of broken homes and/or physically abusive parents. These studies have rarely mentioned, let alone measured, the degree of deprivation of physical affection, although this is often inferred from the degree of neglect and abuse. One exceptional study in this respect is that of Brandt F. Steele and C. B. Pollock who studied child abuse in three generations of families who physically abused their children. They found that parents who abused their children were invariably deprived of physical affection themselves during childhood and that their adult sex life was extremely poor. Steele noted that almost without exception the women who abused their children had never experienced orgasm. The degree of sexual pleasure experienced by the men who abused their children was not ascertained, but their sex life, in general, was unsatisfactory. The hypothesis that physical pleasure actively inhibits physical violence can be appreciated from our own sexual experiences. How many of us feel like assaulting someone after we have just experienced orgasm?

The contributions of Freud to the effects of early experiences upon later behaviors and the consequences of repressed sexuality have been well established ...

The hypothesis that deprivation of physical pleasure results in physical violence requires a formal systematic evaluation. We can test this hypothesis by examining crosscultural studies of child-rearing practices, sexual behaviors, and physical violence. We would expect to find that human societies which provide their infants and children with a great deal of physical affection (touching, holding, carrying) would be less physically violent than human societies which give very little physical affection to their infants and children. Similarly, human societies which tolerate and accept premarital and extra-marital sex would be less physically violent than societies which prohibit and punish premarital and extramarital sex ...

... Those societies which give their infants the greatest amount of physical affection were characterized by low theft, low infant physical pain, low religious activity, and negligible or absent killing, mutilating, or torturing of the enemy. These data directly confirm that the deprivation of body pleasure during infancy is significantly linked to a high rate of crime and violence.

Some societies physically punish their infants as a matter of discipline, while others do not. We can determine whether this punishment reflects a general concern for the infant's welfare by matching it against child nurturant care. The results indicate that societies which inflict pain and discomfort upon their infants tend to neglect them as well ...

... Child rearing practices do not predict patterns of later sexual behavior .... Six societies characterized by both high infant affection and high

violence were compared in terms of their premarital sexual behavior....
Apparently, the social customs which influence and determine the behaviors of sexual affection are different from those which underlie the expression of physical affection toward infants... Five of the six societies exhibited premarital sexual repression, where virginity was a high value of the
cultures. It appears that *the beneficial effects of infant physical affection can
be negated by the repression of physical pleasure (premarital sex) later in
life.*

The seven societies characterized by both low infant physical affection
and low adult physical violence were all found to be characterized by
permissive premarital sexual behaviors. Thus, *the detrimental effects of
infant physical affectional deprivation seem to be compensated for later in
life by sexual body pleasure experiences during adolescence.*

... In short, violence may stem from deprivation of somatosensory pleasure either in infancy or in adolescence.... When physical affection and
pleasure during adolescence as well as in infancy are related to measures
of violence, we find direct evidence of a significant relationship between
the punishment of premarital sex behaviors and various measures of crime
and violence.[34]

Thus the displacement of human sexual needs expresses itself in bizarre and violent ways, and children are often the
victims.

✎ Prescott also contends that violence as a chain reaction can
be broken when fathers teach their daughters to be more nurturing, and when mothers teach their sons to be more nurturing to females. The role of the father is crucial in patriarchal
cultures because, while the mother is usually the primary car-
rier of nurturance in the family, the father is more often the
one to set the affectional tone. If the father is low in nurturance, even if the mother is very nurturing, the family as a
whole will have a low level in this regard. However, if the
father is a very nurturing figure, the family will tend to be high
in nurturance regardless of the mother's nurturing capacity.

TYPICAL CASE PROFILE

AGE	one month
SEX	male
ASSAILANT	mother
RECENT EXTERNAL INJURIES	small contusions — face and head
FRACTURES	ribs — recent
INTERNAL INJURIES	contusions — brain, heart and lungs
CAUSE OF DEATH	contusions — brain, heart and lungs
PRESENTING STORY	"found dead in crib"
METHOD OF INJURY	struck with hand
REASON FOR INJURY	excessive crying

CHAPTER 3
The Other Parent and Society

A child has been battered by one of its parents. The other parent has either witnessed this behaviour or is aware of it because of the bruises, welts or other injuries. The other parent often knows what is happening.* Why does this adult remain silent? Why does this person not come to the defence of the child?

The answers to these questions lie in the particular relationship that exists between the parents of the battered child. Case findings indicate that the other parent usually makes no attempt, or at best only a feeble, half-hearted one, to protect the child. The other parent is often extremely insecure about what it means to be a parent and may also have a rigid authoritarian attitude about child rearing. The other parent usually goes

---

*Gil found that in 30% of 1,380 reported cases of child abuse the other parent or parent-substitute was present during the incident; other adult members of the household in 5.9%; and adults from outside the household in 8.2% of the cases. Other children from the same household were present in 62.2% of the cases, thus not only witnessing the terrifying and traumatic events, but also experiencing the demonstration of violence as a method of child rearing.[1]

along with the actions of the battering parent and often may unwittingly encourage them.[2-4] He or she may feel that the punitive parent is taking the regrettable but nevertheless necessary and correct measure in attempting to make this child obey.

The question still remains, however, how it is possible for a person to observe the terror on the face of a child or to hear the screams of pain from a child, and still not respond. The answer to this question is as important as the discussion of the psychopathology of the battering parent. For the acceptance of the act of battering by the other parent reveals a tolerance of violence against children in our culture, and discloses the larger horror implicit in the Battered Child Syndrome.

North American society has not decided what is the correct way to bring up children. If society has made any decisions at all, they usually fall on the side of physical punishment as the dominant child-rearing method. If children do not learn, then one must be harsh. If children do not respond, one must be punitive. If children do not obey, one must strike them.[5,6]

The parent who permits battering, along with the battering parent, adheres to the *extreme* of an attitude which is commonly held by many otherwise normal people who accept, to one degree or another, the right of society to perpetrate *any* attack so long as it is done under the guise of *punishment in the service of authority*.[7] Physical punishment is seen as a regrettable but nevertheless *correct* way of dealing with children. Anyone who does not recognize corporal punishment as the correct way, is seen as causing a potential delinquent to be fostered, or at least allowing all sorts of more subtle, wicked and wanton habits to develop in the child. That is, the child will grow up to be slovenly, ill-mannered, crime-ridden and morally depraved if corporal discipline is not maintained.[8]

If asked about the justice of child beating the public responds with horror. It is a very wicked thing to do. But, in the next breath, these same people respond differently if child beating as a form of punishment is linked to obedience. The public, the law, the school, the church and the politician all want to know what punishment does this or that particular act deserve? What is the correct and right punishment to give a child who commits this act or does not obey that rule? Society, by accepting that corporal punishment as a right and necessary response to misbehaviour, sets the stage for all kinds of atrocities.

What the society wants to know is, what did the child do? It is unfortunate that he was punished, but tell us, what did he do to deserve the punishment? Then we will judge whether or not it was right and proper for the child to have been punished. It is not that physical assault is a bad thing; it is only seen as bad if it "went too far" or if the child did not deserve to be punished. This philosophical attitude of society has to be examined before child battering and the deferring parent can be understood.[9]

The public feels that it is all well and good to talk about not striking children, but it cannot accept that there are any workable alternatives. This is the slippery slide which leads the public away from the issue of child battering and down into the whole murky area of punishment and child rearing in general. Legislators are aware that the public can become very defensive and angry when faced with anything that threatens to weaken parental authority. Perhaps that is why legislators have been so reluctant to tackle the reality of overall child abuse as it exists.

The public asks what will happen if parents have even fewer rights than they do now to carry out their functions as a parent (i.e. to punish). This question reflects society's confusion. The good life and a happy family are not attainable by the striking of children. On the contrary, if society wants its children to be gentle, kind, easy-going, fair, honest, creative, happy and good-natured, then parents must set this example themselves. There is no way we can punish people into learning. Most importantly, there is no way we can punish people into obeying unless we stand guard over them day and night: that is, virtually enslave them.

Society has developed a method of child-rearing based on physical punishment and is now reaping the harvest. Our culture, with its punitive child-rearing methods in the home and the school, and its glorification of violence in the media, maintains a high level of aggressiveness in North American society which manifests itself all too clearly in foreign policy.[10]

We have a society which must now face the fact that adults are among the major killers of children. The terrible reality is that many parents are not only failures, but lethal failures. The alternative to facing this realization can only be an increase in the number of children that will be killed and permanently maimed by parents this year, next year and in the years to come. There is no question but that our methods of child rearing are linked to our methods of making war, our methods of conquest, and to the way in which we view people of different coloured skins and different ethnic backgrounds.[11]

Children who have been abused grow up to be violent. Sometimes they are abused by an older brother or sister, sometimes by neighbourhood bullies, sometimes by a baby-sitter. These children, unless protected, become disturbed and often withdrawn or destructive of people or property.

TYPICAL CASE PROFILE

AGE	two years
SEX	female
ASSAILANT	stepfather
RECENT EXTERNAL INJURIES	many bruises and abrasions over face, scalp, and trunk
FRACTURES	ribs, recent
INTERNAL INJURIES	contusion, brain; subdural hemorrhage
CAUSE OF DEATH	subdural hemorrhage
PRESENTING STORY	"fell from bed and downstairs"
METHOD OF INJURY	beat with hair brush
REASON FOR INJURY	child had diarrhea for one week and messed bed

CHAPTER 4
Can Anyone Be a Child Abuser?

After spending time trying to get individuals and organizations to take action in the area of the abused child, one realizes that there is grave underlying guilt on the part of the ordinary citizen about the question of battered and abused children. He feels guilty about not doing anything to help the situation, and guilty too about his own possible involvement as a potential abuser.

There is a belief in North America that anyone could be a child abuser, and that no matter how kind and nice a parent or parents may be under normal circumstances, if they are put under enough pressure they will abuse their children.[1] It is believed that otherwise good-natured, easy-going parents will assault a child as a result of pressures from overwork, worry, conflict, and traumas from other areas. Because it is believed that *anyone* could, under certain circumstances, attack their children, many people feel threatened by a discussion of the subject.

There is no evidence to indicate that all people are potential child abusers. There is no evidence to support the supposition that given enough pressure, tension and trauma a man or woman will turn upon his or her young and strike out. On the contrary, anthropological evidence makes it very clear that whole civilizations, whole groups of people under the most terrible stresses, deprivations and frustrations, have not and would not lash out at their young.[2-6] *A very important immediate task, if we want to reduce the incidence of child battering, is to challenge the widespread belief in our culture that child abuse in times of stress is "normal" or "human nature."*

S. R. Zalba, commenting on what appears to be a lack of awareness of incidents of child abuse, asks:

> Is there any mother or father who has not been "provoked" almost to the breaking point by the crying, wheedling child? How many parents have not had moments of concern and self-recrimination after having, in anger, hit their own child much harder than they expected they would? How many such incidents make a "child abuser" out of a normal parent? There may be a tacit agreement among us not to meddle in each others' private matters unless it is simply impossible to ignore the behaviour involved.[7]

Even in our North American culture, where people are trained and told to believe that it is the right, indeed the duty, of parents to punish children physically, there is no uniformity as to how they will react to children under stressful situations. It is not true that everyone is a potential child abuser; it is not true that if you place enough stress on individuals they will take out their frustrations on their children. It is only true that some people will react this way, and that some of these who will don't need a tremendous amount of stress placed on them in order to vent their hostility upon children.[8]

Child abuse is abnormal behaviour which can no longer be dismissed as a regrettable but inevitable aspect of human nature. Instead, the inside mechanisms, as well as the cultural mechanics that create and maintain a structure of child abuse, must be investigated.

A child batterer is a particular kind of person: a person who is without empathy for the child and who is therefore unable to see the child as a human being. Lacking the ability to identify or empathize with others, these people are able to perpetrate on the child any kind of atrocity with almost as little feeling as they would have if they kicked a chair. The dominant cohesive factor in the child batterer's personality, whether rich, poor, intelligent or stupid, is a lack of identification with the child as a human being. He cannot feel for the child.[9-11] Furthermore, he does not understand the limitations or capabilities of childhood. This is far more subtle and difficult to understand than the actions of someone who is mentally ill and does an injurious act or a series of injurious acts out of complete disturbance and inability to remain in touch with reality.

The average child abuser is in touch with reality, does his or her job well and is, in most ways, an ordinary kind of person functioning quite well in the everyday business of life. It is only behind closed doors that the full extent of this individual's inability to relate to other human beings comes to light. Behind the closed doors of the home the child abuser has full authority and is faced with situations that call forth responses demanding identification with his or her child. Within the family structure, the needs for love and appropriate responses emerge, and the child abuser is unable to understand these needs. For example, child abusers often react violently to a cry which cannot immediately be stopped and is interpreted as an insult and a threat to their authority. If the child does not stop crying they may strike it.

In our everyday social world it is possible for people to avoid intimate emotional contact. It is therefore possible for men and women to appear to others to be perfectly normal and never exposed as the kind of people who, although they may be excellent providers or housekeepers, are nevertheless completely incapable of understanding the needs of children.[12]

Child abusers have in common not only a particular emotional quality (the inability to feel sympathy), but also a philosophical attitude. Child abusers, even though they come from different walks of life, different religious backgrounds and different classes, *almost all appear to hold a hardcore belief in authoritarianism. That is, a dominant belief that authority within the home must never be challenged.*[13]

The child abuser, male or female, often believes that you must not allow children to get away with anything. The child comes into the world more or less as an enemy who must be overcome. The child will automatically be spoiled if the parent does not take vigorous steps to educate him; there is a right way and a wrong way of doing things; the child will be naughty because it is predisposed to do so and it is the job of the parent to take a firm stand on all things. Child abusers believe that they must make immediate demands on a child so that he or she will grow up to be a "good" boy or girl and subsequently a good citizen.[14]

The key to understanding child abusers lies not only in understanding their inability to feel, but also in understanding their inability to comprehend the difference between limits, goals, authority, and punishment. These parents lack the ability to recognize that the infant or small child is not capable of understanding authority or demands inappropriate to its age. Because the child abuser cannot identify with children, he or she cannot understand why, for example, a child, at the age of two weeks or a month, cannot respond to the complicated structure that is involved in the command, "stop crying." The child abuser does not understand that the child is incapable of responding at an adult level.[15] No matter what the age of the child, the abusing parent demands an immediate response to all commands. If the child *cannot* or does not respond to that demand, the reaction on the part of the parent is often violent.

Many people have conflicts with children who are difficult. The normal person faced with a colicky, crotchety infant is confused and certainly worried that something might be wrong with the infant. The normal parent may attempt to make the infant eat because, in good faith, he or she feels that the infant should eat. But when the child makes it clear that it does not want to eat, the normal parent assumes that it is unwise to force the child. In other words, the normal parent does not experience the child's refusal of food as a threat to his or her authority, but rather as a situation which is difficult and unpleasant for both of them. The normal parent does not feel that the child is particularly disposed to some sort of inner wickedness. The normal parent may definitely be confused about what is going on because interpreting a small child's needs is often difficult and confusing. However, the dominant factor in the interactions is their basic empathy. That is, their ability to feel for the small child and to have sympathy for the child's dilemma. It is this ability, whether in males or females, that constitutes the nurturing quality.

In this culture, even normal parents are very often poorly trained in dealing with children. However, by living through situations, understanding and coping with them, normal parents gain an increased knowledge and insight into what parenthood is all about. Perhaps as an aside one might say that the reason why people often become better parents as they go along is that, as many are heard to say, "we made our worst mistakes on the first child." Strangely enough a corollary of this bit of common wisdom is that parents tend to be more lenient with children as they go along. So if there is any cultural insight into what it means to be a parent, it appears to be learning how to be kinder and more easy-going with children, as well as being more sensitive and understanding of their needs and desires.

Joe Jacobs, Chairman of the Mental Health Committee of the Canadian Paediatric Society, in his excellent volume *Child Abuse, Neglect, Deprivation and the Family Syndrome*, reminds us that the degree of violence separating so-called normal parents from abusers is often merely a question of cultural definition regarding abusive behaviour. In many cultures the thought of striking a child is odious.

However, Jacobs notes that:

> Studies in the U.S.A. and England show that between 84 percent and 97 percent of all parents use physical punishment at some point in their child's life.[16] A West German poll showed that up to 60 percent of parents believe in beating (not slapping or spanking, but beating) their children. Parents not uncommonly strap toddlers into cribs and leave them alone without baby sitters. Child abuse is not unusual. "We beat our children dumb in this nation."[17] Christine Danat, a consulting psychologist in Paris[18] writes that, "Discipline is such a part of a French child's life, from the earliest age of strictly regular feeding, through a military routine at nursery school and certainly until the beginning of secondary education, that it is generally accepted." Corporal punishment and severe curtailment of privileges (a family may go on vacation without taking a misbehaving child) enforce diligent work habits.[19]

AGE	six years
SEX	female
ASSAILANT	sibling (age twelve)
RECENT EXTERNAL INJURIES	many bruises on head and trunk
FRACTURES	none
INTERNAL INJURIES	laceration of spleen
CAUSE OF DEATH	laceration of spleen with hemorrhage
PRESENTING STORY	"fell from toilet seat"
METHOD OF INJURY	struck with vacuum cleaner pipe and fists
REASON FOR INJURY	was leaning out window

CHAPTER 5
Battering in a Middle Class Family

Consider a middle class family in which there is a permitting father, a battering mother and two small children. The first child, aged five, is regarded as relatively well-behaved. The second child, Bobby, aged two, is felt by both parents to be a difficult child. Bobby was fussy as an infant and gave his parents considerable trouble at mealtime. Since infancy the mother's treatment of the child has been harsh and demanding. In the course of several conflicts the infant was battered. During the two years of his life, in addition to the physical things which have been done to him, Bobby has also been emotionally deprived. He seldom received smiles, strokes or cuddles and, although he has received some affection from his father, over all Bobby has not enjoyed the warmth and approval which constitute nurturing. His mother is almost constantly irked and irritated by him. She makes her general disapproval towards the child clear by her body movements, her facial expressions, and her tone of voice.

There is, nevertheless, a concern on the part of the mother for her second child. She wants him to be good, to be healthy and, above all, to be a credit to her. As a result of her concern, she takes Bobby to her pediatrician. She explains that he is difficult and won't eat. The pediatrician checks Bobby in his office. Bobby has a few bruises on his arms and is a pound or two underweight, but otherwise appears to be a normal, healthy child. Nevertheless the mother is still very concerned about the child's eating. In order to soothe the mother's concern, and just to be on the safe side, the pediatrician puts Bobby in the hospital. Once Bobby is hospitalized the mother has little interest in his condition and the parents seldom come to visit him during his stay.

When the pediatrician made his office examination, he noted some bruises. From x-rays taken as part of the hospital examination, he now discovers that the child suffered several fractures in the past which do not appear on his medical record.

If the physician is conversant with the literature on battered children, the behaviour of both the child and the parents during the child's stay in the hospital will further verify a suspected case of child battering. A five-year study of abused children and their parents notes that there are characteristic patterns of behaviour exhibited by both child and parents.[1]

Once Bobby has settled into the hospital, he is quite content to be without his parents. This is in contrast to most children who cling to their parents when they are brought in and who turn to them for comfort and assurance throughout the examination and treatment. These children show, by word and action, that they want their parents to be there with them, are reassured by their parents' visits, and want to go home as soon as possible.

Although battered children may cry under treatment and examination, in general they cry very little and do not look to their parents for reassurance. They are wary of physical contact initiated either by a parent or an attending person, and they often become apprehensive when adults approach another crying child. They have a look about them which makes one feel that they are constantly on the alert for danger, and may assume a flat, expressionless appearance when any mention of returning home is made. In general, well-nurtured children turn to their parents for safety in life, while battered children bear up under life as if they are alone in a dangerous world with no hope of any safety.

35

In the hospital, Bobby thrives. He eats well, sleeps well and seems perfectly happy and content to be without his parents. The pediatrician, noting this, will suspect that any feeding problems Bobby has must result from conflict in the home.[2]

Based on case studies, it can be said that the pediatrician may respond in several ways.[3] Because Bobby is a middle-class child it may not enter his mind that Bobby's fractures could be linked to battering. Even if he strongly suspects abuse he may still be confused about his role and believe that he would have to determine the guilt of either parent before he could report the case to the authorities. As a result the pediatrician may feel that his suspicions are not sufficient when weighed against the parents' fury which might arise if he were to question them about possible child abuse.

As a pediatrician, he should know that children who are once battered run a very high risk of being severely battered again,[4,5] and that the Battered Child Syndrome constitutes a major killer of children.

From statistics in this area, it is clear that too few pediatricians press the parents about the cause of the previous fractures.[6,7] Too few question the mother in depth about her attitude towards the child, and recommend that she seek advice from a psychologist, a psychiatrist, or a social agency.[8]

After Bobby has been seen by the doctor the mother does attempt to ease up on the problem. She develops some sort of ritual which she now decides will get them both over the business of eating. Nevertheless, the mother continues to have a high level of irritation and aggression toward the child, particularly at meals, which continue to be a time of conflict between them. This tension often results in erratic bursts of violence on the part of the mother during or around meal times.

The second major area of conflict between the mother and the child centres on toilet training.[9] Bobby's mother attempted to train him early, but at the age of three he still wets his bed. Although this is not unusual for a three-year-old, his bedwetting drives the mother frantic. She tries any number of routines to cope with this. She does not allow him to drink anything past a certain hour. She punishes him by shaming and embarrassing him in front of other children, in front of his father and in front of relatives. She calls him a baby. She calls him dumb and stupid. She flies into furious rages and often beats the child. And every morning there is the dreaded examination to find out whether the child has or has not once again wet his bed. So mornings also are a time of great conflict.

As Bobby grows older and the problem still persists, the mother's fury increases and she continues periodically to beat, slap, scratch, pinch, shove, and hurl the child about in an expression of her rage at the child's inability to obey her. The mother has ordered this child not to wet its bed and it consistently disobeys her. To the mother this means that the child is purposely trying to thwart her; purposely pointing out her impotence. The child is winning; she is losing. She has to clean up the wet sheets and she hates and loathes this child. Of course this child hates and loathes her, although the child still wants and needs her love and is dependent upon her.

The child is not allowed to display any anger or resentment towards her because she is, of course, acting only in his own good. It is right and proper that this ungrateful child learn to stop wetting his bed, and the only thing that he must display towards her is obedience, gratitude and love.

During a particular blow-up scene over bed-wetting, Bobby is severely beaten and flung across the room. As a result of this incident he develops a headache and fever. The mother becomes worried and again takes Bobby to the pediatrician. Bobby is a bit older now and once again the pediatrician examines him, finding nothing seriously wrong. There are bruises on the child but the mother explains that they occurred when he fell off his tricycle. The pediatrician does not ask any further questions about these bruises. Although he suspects that there is difficulty between the mother and child, he tells himself that situations like this are unfortunate, but not the kind of thing he feels he can get involved with, and besides, most children are covered with bruises a fair amount of the time just in the normal course of living.

The mother once again explains to the pediatrician that she is distraught. She is convinced that there is something deeply wrong with Bobby because he consistently wets his bed. The pediatrician prescribes various medications and has another little talk with the mother, soothing her and pointing out that the child will undoubtedly grow out of this. He tells her not to worry because bed-wetting is a normal occurrence in children of this age. This child is his patient, but once again he does not take this opportunity to question the mother about her relationship with the child. He does not question the mother as to what might be taking place at home. Why should he? As far as he is concerned this is just another child with a bed-wetting problem.

If he suspected that Bobby had any *physical* disease he would run a battery of tests. If he suspected that the child were allergic, or that there might be any disorder in his physical health, he would send Bobby to any number of other child specialists. Why does he not send the mother and the child to a child psychiatrist or, if he has sufficient reason, report this case to the child welfare authorities? One reason appears to be that he does not want to get involved.[10,11] He does not want to interfere with the personal relationship between the mother and the child. Possibly another is that he mistakenly assumes that the parent rather than the child is his patient, and that the details of the case are therefore confidential. A third possibility is that, rightly or wrongly, the physician may feel that little or no action will follow such a report.[12] It is difficult to conceive, however, of a physician failing to report a case of diphtheria because of difficulties in providing treatment. The responsibility of the physician is surely to fulfil his diagnostic function to the best of his ability. Any doubts about the efficiency of the follow-up services should have no effect on this duty.

This is the second time that the pediatrician has had an opportunity to recommend that the mother seek help in the emotional conflict between herself and the child, or to investigate more fully Bobby's medical history of fractures and bruises. However, pediatricians and doctors are notoriously poor at reporting child abuse even though it is known that the children involved, if sent home, continue to live in an atmosphere of conflict, violence and hatred.

> If he [the physician] does not accept the responsibility, twenty-five to thirty percent of the time the child will be permanently injured or killed within the next several months.[13-15]

A few weeks after her visit to the pediatrician the mother abuses Bobby in another violent episode. She realizes that he should receive immediate medical attention, but is confused about what to do. Instead of taking any immediate action, she simply puts it off – she does not respond.

When the father returns home, he realizes that they should do something. The parents call their pediatrician and are told that he is on vacation. They are advised to take the child to a hospital. Both parents take Bobby to the emergency ward of a major hospital in their city, where they claim that he was injured in a fall down a flight of stairs. Bobby's parents, like most discussed in the literature on battered children, are anxious to leave the hospital as quickly as possible, and show little interest in his progress.[16]

Bobby is treated by an attending doctor who finds many welts and bruises on his body and suspects that he has been beaten. After seeing the child's x-ray plates and after consultation with a radiologist, the doctor recognizes Bobby as a battered child. However, after approaching his senior staff members with this information, the attending physician is dissuaded from taking any action because the senior staff member does not want to become involved, and because there is no hospital procedure for these matters. Literature documents case after case in which a child's life was forfeited because physicians did not take effective measures to prevent further incidents.[17-21]

From conversations with workers in Canadian hospitals, it is apparent that this a fairly common occurrence. Incidents often occur in which battered children are treated in the hospital, recognized as battered children, but the physician in charge makes no report to the provincial child welfare authorities. Therefore, many cases are never reported by hospitals as battering incidents.

Since most Canadian hospitals seldom report battering cases to provincial agencies for investigation, Bobby, when he is well enough, is automatically returned home to his parents.* This occurs in spite of the fact that study after study indicates that once abuse has taken place, the occurrence of a second and third episode is almost inevitable, since only a small percentage of cases are isolated occurrences. Children who are subjected to such patterns of abuse run a great risk of being permanently injured or killed. The hospital and physician have placed this child in an extremely hazardous situation by returning him to the home.

Within a short time Bobby is brought back to the hospital unconscious, and he dies of further injuries.[23] Again the parents say the injuries were caused by a fall, this time from a swing. An autopsy reveals that, while Bobby died as a result of a massive blow to the head, he also had many large bruises on

*Reports are more likely to be made in cases involving poor families than in cases involving middle or upper class children.[22]

his body and several old, healing fractures which in no way are accounted for in the parents' story. However, in view of the parents' position in the community, nothing further is done. The case is closed and the cause of Bobby's death accepted as a blow received while playing on a swing.[24]

Although the above is a hypothetical case, it is quite typical of many middle class battering deaths.[25]

AGE	two months
SEX	male
ASSAILANT	father
RECENT EXTERNAL INJURIES	single bruise over lower sternum
FRACTURES	none
INTERNAL INJURIES	laceration of liver
CAUSE OF DEATH	laceration of liver with hemorrhage
PRESENTING STORY	"fell from lap"
METHOD OF INJURY	threw feeding bottle at baby
REASON FOR INJURY	would not finish feeding

CHAPTER 6
Needed: A Model for Parenthood

There are parents who, having been abused as children,[1] recognize that they have been deprived of love and warm human contact, and educate themselves about providing their own children with these necessities. They attempt to deal with their conscious and unconscious authoritarian drives, sometimes so successfully that they actually acquire the empathy, warmth, and understanding that were missing from their own childhood. Parenthood is a difficult experience for these people, for they have had no model on which to base their handling of their children. As a result, in attempting to provide the love and kindness that they never had, they may find it difficult to set limits for their children. They tend to provide too much, or try to become too involved in their children's lives. This sometimes leads to situations in which these parents find themselves being bullied by their own children. During the growing-up period of their children they may, because of their inability to understand what is a reasonable and what is an unreasonable demand, over-indulge their children and allow them to become spoiled, greedy or manipulating.

Such a parent, who was emotionally or physically abused as a child, is in a very complicated and difficult position. This person may reject not only his authoritarian background, but also the authoritarianism of the culture around him. He may try to develop an alternate way of life based on kindness and gentleness. The difficulty arises, however, in the fact that so little in society supports gentleness. On the contrary, in our society gentleness is equated with weakness. Gentleness in males is regarded as effeminate and therefore to be ridiculed and despised; while in women, gentleness often elicits bullying and exploitation. Unlike the battered child grownup who in turn batters his children and does so with a solemn conviction that what he does is correct, and who finds substantiation for this in the attitudes of society, this person is unable to find a cultural model of how to be strong and at the same time gentle. He lacks the usable pattern of behaviour towards children that most people learn from observing their parents' reactions. For them most transactions must be taken on in isolation. There is no precedent for their behaviour in their past and, as a result, they have to tackle and think their way through each situation.

Sometimes these people find that the odds are just too great or that they lack the emotional strength needed to see them through challenging situations. In encounters with authoritarians, perhaps employers, sales clerks, friends, husbands, wives or even their own children, they may find themselves very vulnerable and easily bullied. So much in our society supports the authoritarian structure that its victims, and those who reject it for other reasons, find very little support for their position in the everyday business of living.

Further, they may have inner difficulties insofar as they are often emotionally crippled and may suffer from what R. D. Laing refers to as ontological insecurity.[2] They are insecure because during their formative years, when they should have learned security and that their immediate environment was a safe and good one, they learned on the contrary that there was no security and that their environment, far from being safe, was in fact hostile.

As adults, they have had to create for themselves or find by chance that which allows them to function reasonably and with some degree of stability. This means that they are unable to take on the culture, the society, or an authoritarian structure in a rational way. They are often left wondering what is the right thing to do. They feel that warmth, kindness and permissiveness is more correct than aggressiveness and cold authoritarianism, yet it is very difficult for them to find the appropriate models necessary to become the parents they would like to be. As a result, thrown on their own devices, these parents often make the mistake of being indecisive about their role as parents. They expect their children to act as parents to them. This in turn may make their children feel insecure because they are left without definite limits.

An additional characteristic in these parents is that they often have difficulty in understanding their own capabilities and limits. Because of the extremely high demands of their own parents upon them, they may continue to over-demand of themselves throughout their adult life and may, as a result, overwork themselves. Or they may become martyrish and express the feeling that they work so hard but without any appreciation. This combination of impossibly high demands on themselves, coupled with their martyrdom, may make other family members feel both confused and guilty.

Another example of battered, abused or emotionally deprived children grown-up are the adults who, in their home life and in their functions as wives or husbands, may be quite authoritarian and yet unable to recognize it. While they do not batter their children, their violent temper is just under the surface at all times. Constantly monitoring everything that goes on, they are rarely pleased with anything or able to find pleasure or satisfaction in their own lives. This makes them extremely difficult to live with. As a result they often cause their families to be insecure. These people are usually extremely restless and often lack the ability to be warm and affectionate. They do not, as a rule, violently beat their children, but on occasion they may strike them quite hard, and they usually maintain strict discipline in the family. These are the kind of people who are often charming and successful in their everyday lives, but whose attitude is one of self-indulgence and authoritarianism at home. They are inclined to stand on their position as "the mother" or "the father," and feel that everything should revolve around them. They often choose spouses who defer to their role. Everything is subservient to their goals, wishes, demands and desires. As a rule they rarely bother to question their own attitudes, reactions or treatment of their family, although they may be quite opposed to what they perceive as authoritarianism in society.

These parents often force their children, by their unrealistic expectations and increasing demands, to make a choice of either becoming like them and joining forces with them, or facing complete rejection. They allow no middle ground for any kind of interaction, and present each demand in a manner that makes it clear to the child that unless it does exactly as the parent wants and commands it will receive the total disapproval of the parent.

This is the opposite of the parent who over-indulges the child in a love-guilt relationship. These over-demanding parents are, on the contrary, without guilt. Instead of over-indulging they are quick to reject the child and to disown it emotionally.

These are two very brief descriptions of abused children grown-up who do not indulge in physical battering of their children. Often recognizing themselves as potential child abusers, they intellectually reject the authoritarian structure in society which so completely supports the traditionally battering parent. However, no matter how hard they try intellectually to reject their emotional authoritarianism, there is always the phantom of the brutal reactions which were taught so thoroughly by their parents, threatening to erupt when stressful situations arise. It is not unusual therefore to find these types of parents suddenly bursting out in irrational fits of temper, thus reverting back to the experience of their own childhood.

The difference between these parents and the battering parent is that these people suffer terrible remorse and guilt as a result of these outbursts. They feel guilty because they have no philosophical structure to support this kind of action. While one abused child grows up to batter with impunity and does so with no remorse whatsoever, and may even be cross with the child for having managed to get itself injured, these other parents, having struck a child, are filled with remorse and despair.

The society does not provide any education about how to be parents. Those who have had an abusive parent model have to learn for themselves and often at the expense of their children, whom they really love and cherish, how to avoid perpetrating the same abuses as were enacted on them. Often these people, unlike battering parents, see their own parents as victims in a cycle of abuse, and are able to have warm and loving feelings towards them even though they are aware of the parent's short-comings. They understand very well the difficulties that their own parents experienced in raising them.

By failing to provide a clear alternative to punitive and authoritarian child-rearing practices, society abandons not only the abused child and the abusing parent, but also the non-abusing parent who does not know what is the right thing to do. For adult sons and daughters of abusive parents, professional help and self-analysis are certainly the obvious requisites for insight into their problems.

People want their children to be the subjects of their own personal experiments. If they succeed, all is well; if they don't, it is the child who is seen to be the failure. This is the dominant attitude in the North American culture and it will certainly remain the dominant attitude unless a hard look is taken at what it means to be a human being. There is not a great margin for error in the treatment of human beings. It has been assumed that people can do practically anything with children. Actually, there are just a very few ways that people can treat children and have them grow up to be healthy, sane individuals.

Tracing childhood experiences into the womb reveals that children are at risk from parents who, for whatever reason, do not want them or are not fit to bear or nurture them. No amount of sentimentality on the part of those who believe in the right to life will change the grisly toll of children maimed through parental rejection. States, religious groups, or lobbyists, as has been shown historically, cannot legislate love. Mothers who, during their pregnancy, do not care for their own health, who smoke, drink, take tranquilizers, or any combination of drugs prescribed or sold over the counter, also place their children at serious risk. Increasing evidence pours in regarding the vulnerability of the fetus to radioactive particles, x-rays, alcohol, drugs, and pollutants of all categories, including such common things as aspirin and coffee.

A child who is not placed with its mother at the time of birth does not bond with that mother. The most recent scientific data supports this position. The child lies abandoned, and in fact appears to go into a form of loss or grieving. The need for constant attention to the infant rests on the fact that the human child is born, unlike many other animals, completely dependent on the mother, and appears to make a bond with that mother that sets the tone for its mental and physical development. It is obvious that the human infant does not need a doctor or a nurse; that what the baby needs is its mother. But no money can be made from this experience. Hence, it was a common practice in Canada to keep the mother's legs together until the doctor could deliver the baby, and that was so up until not too many years ago.

Outstanding research by Klaus and Kennell[3] has provided important and essential data that gives researchers on child abuse and violence direct insight into the importance of parental-infant bonding. To a large degree the lack of parental-infant bonding explains why parents abandon, abuse, and otherwise fail to protect their offspring. Klaus and Kennell's work enlarges on Bowlby's[4] findings that for optimum growth the child must be loved.

As Harry Harlow noted in 1959: "Affection in infants was long thought to be generated by the satisfactions of feeding. Studies of young rhesus monkeys now indicate that love derives mainly from close bodily contact."[5]

Psychoanalyst Sandor Rado, in 1931, suggested that an important element in early sucking lies in the achievement of a pleasant feeling of satiety and a diffuse feeling of sensual pleasure in which the whole organism participates, and he described this as an "alimentary orgasm."[6]

The human child must be affectionately and constantly nurtured. This need for nurturing is consistent with all small animals and is related to growth, and has many important and long-ranging effects on maturity and sexual development.

Children need and must have calm, loving, consistent relationships with the individuals who are around them.[7] After the age of three the concept that one dominant parent, the mother, should be solely responsible for the care of the child, is being questioned. This questioning is substantiated by cultures where children are loved and nurtured by all the members of the tribe or clan, not just by the parents.[8] Children are secure so long as they are treated kindly and have no reason to assume that they will be treated in anything other than a kind manner. On the basis of experience they will, without fear, sit on as many knees as are offered. They will be petted by as many hands as wish to pet. They will smile at as many smiling faces as appear. Children are amazingly plastic in the amount of love and affection they can accept. There is no reason to think that children have to be bound solely to one mother and one father in order to be secure. Children are made secure by the love they experience in the transactions that take place in their lives. A wretchedly poor emotional environment, even if it does not batter, can kill or permanently maim children.[9,10]

The Minister of National Health and Welfare, in his December 16th, 1975 presentation to the Parliamentary Standing Committee on Health, Welfare and Social Affairs, stated that we might look toward the following:

> 1. Increased emphasis in our educational system on realistic and practical courses for young persons, both male and female, on subjects such as child rearing and child care, family life, marriage, responsibilities of parenthood, homemaking and management of finances.
> 2. The development of children's centres, offering health and social services, including pre-natal care, to pre-school children and their parents. Such centres have been established in other countries, most notably Denmark, for the purposes of prevention, early detection, and correction of medical and social problems, including neglect and abuse of children.
> 3. Wider dissemination of information to the general public as well as the helping professions. This information should include two major elements: (i) when, how, what, and to whom to report actual or potential child abuse and neglect, and (ii) what can be expected to happen after a report is made. (Under the latter heading, people should be told that the Child Welfare authority must and will investigate and take appropriate action, which usually will include the assistance of a multi-disciplinary team of specialists, that the neglectful parents will not necessarily face prison or even separation from their children, and that the person reporting does not risk legal reprisals unless the information is given maliciously.) Beyond this, the mass media might be used as an effective force for publicizing and promoting "good" family life, as the B.B.C. has attempted to do.[11]

These suggestions are logical and essential. However, when these programs will actually come into effect is another matter.

Increasingly, more people are concerned about the traditional rights of parents. Roger W. McIntire, writing in *Psychology Today*, said: "Screening and selecting potential parents would by no means guarantee that they would in fact be good parents. Today, however, we have almost no means of ensuring proper child-rearing methods. The indiscriminate 'right to parent' enables everyone, however ill-equipped, to practice any parental behavior they please. Very often their behavior would be illegal if applied to any group other than children. But because of our prejudice against the rights of children, we protect parents unless the most savage and brutal parental behavior can be proved in court."[12]

The result of this folly we now begin to count in terms of physical abuse, neglect, and emotional impairment.

The Canadian Mental Health Association states that as of January 29th, 1976:

– Mental illness disabled more Canadians than all other illnesses combined.

– Nearly half of the hospital beds in Canada were occupied by the mentally and emotionally ill.

– Psychiatric institutions provided 21 million patient-days of care in 1972.[13]

– 106,211 patients were admitted for treatment in 1972 – a 111 per cent increase since 1962.[14]

– 53,928 patients entered Canadian hospitals for the first time in 1972 – a rate of 260 per 100,000 of population.[15]

– 52,283 patients were readmitted for further treatment in 1972 (the readmission rate has increased 158 per cent over the past ten years).[16]

– 255,107 persons were treated in clinics and outpatient departments in 1973, 39 per cent of whom were attending for the first time.[17]

– The operating expenditure of psychiatric institutions reached $523.8 million in 1973.

– Average cost of per patient day:
– public mental hospitals $31.57
– psychiatric hospitals $64.74
– centres for emotionally disturbed children $154.80[18]

– The total cost of psychiatric services and 84,749 work years lost in the productive age group was at least $1 billion (1971). The estimates for 1974 amount to $1.5 billion.

The indirect costs incurred in rehabilitation, education, welfare, corrections, employment and crisis intervention services were impossible to calculate.[19]

– At least one million children and youth have emotional or learning disorders requiring professional help.[20]

– The number of children admitted to centres for emotionally disturbed children increased by 32.9 per cent between 1962 and 1972 – the largest of any age group.[21]

– One out of every six babies born in 1976 will be admitted for psychiatric treatment during its lifetime.[22]*

– Suicide is now the second most frequent cause of death among young Canadians between the ages of 15 and 30.

– Upwards of one third of the population has suffered some temporary disability because of emotional problems.

– At least 50 per cent of the patients seen in general medical practice suffer from an underlying emotional disorder.

– Some 190,000 serious crimes are committed annually in Canada.

– There are at least 5,000 narcotic addicts and many more dependent on drugs.

– There are at least 250,000 alcoholics in Canada.[23]

*To indicate the conservative nature of the estimate, the Dominion Bureau of Statistics states: "An unknown, presumably quite large number of undetected and untreated persons suffering from mental disorders are excluded from our expectation of admissions table."

Mental illness is now the most urgent health problem in North America.

The problems of the child require the interdisciplinary efforts of many specialists who, by examining human behaviour, will continue to dispel cherished ignorances and fears about touch, sensuality, and nurturing of all kinds. The North American family is ignorant about good child-rearing practices. When men and women are trained to be good fathers and mothers, they will provide not only nurturing but protection for the child.

TYPICAL CASE PROFILE

AGE	seventeen months
SEX	female
ASSAILANT	unknown
RECENT EXTERNAL INJURIES	many bruises over face, neck, and trunk
FRACTURES	ribs — recent
INTERNAL INJURIES	contusions — brain, lungs, and heart
CAUSE OF DEATH	contusions — brain, lungs, and heart
PRESENTING STORY	"fell downstairs"
METHOD OF INJURY	unknown
REASON FOR INJURY	unknown

CHAPTER 7
A New Role for the Physician

In the case of the child Bobby, discussed in Chapter Five, had the pediatrician been conversant with the battered child literature and acted upon this information, he might very well have saved the life of this child.* When the mother first approached the pediatrician it would have been possible to have dealt with the mother's anxiety without alienating her and her husband.

Often these parents approach physicians under the pretext of seeking medical help for the child when in fact they deeply desire help for themselves.[1] Even if the pediatrician did not strongly suspect abuse on the first visit, subsequent developments should have alerted him to the dangers facing the child. When the child was brought to the hospital for the second time, the physician should have kept him there in order to completely assess the case, as well as to protect the child until

---

*Since the first edition of The Battered Child in Canada in 1972, there has been an increase in awareness on the part of medical schools as to the diagnostic, treatment and preventative techniques available to professionals. However, overall the problem is still not included uniformly as part of the general medical or nursing curriculum.

such time as both he and the investigating authority were convinced that releasing the child to the parents was the appropriate action. Generally, admission to hospital is used in order to protect children where abuse is suspected, and it is recommended that this be done even though the actual medical findings may not be sufficient to warrant this.[2]

It is essential that the hospital staff should not antagonize the parents, so that the relationship between the doctor and the parents may continue on a firm basis. The fact that the child is in the hospital allows time for conversation with the parents to take place in a more relaxed manner. If the child is old enough, it also gives the physician an opportunity to question him about what has taken place. This does not mean that the physician's function is to establish guilt, but rather to determine whether the child's environment is unsafe.

Many times parents are frightened by what has taken place and are willing to be quite helpful so long as the doctors and hospital staff are not abusive or threatening. If cases are properly handled from the beginning and no one has antagonized the parents, Dr. R. E. Helfer reports that it is common for parents to be willing and often relieved to admit a child to the hospital. He believes that if the parents are kept well informed of *everything* that goes on and what is found, they are usually willing to leave the child in the hospital until some definite plan can be made. Helfer points out too that most parents of injured children want to be helped. If this help is offered in the absence of any implicit or explicit threats, he says, the parents are usually cooperative.[3]

Every child who has a serious, unexplained injury should have x-rays of the long bones, ribs and skull.[4] This is the physician's most important diagnostic tool and should be utilized in all situations involving the possibly battered child.[5] However, if the child is seen soon after the initial trauma, the evidence of this trauma may be missed on the x-rays. If there is a high suspicion of abuse, x-rays of the long bones should be taken after a two-or three-week period.[6]

The importance of understanding the cumulative dangers of over-radiation, however, requires a continuing check with all the previous medical data. Cooper writes: "A particular emphasis should be put on the need for obtaining previous x-rays, or at least their number and extent, since an appropriate number of x-rays related to the age of the child may also raise the question of abuse. (The provincial health insurance records respecting radiological examination may provide the clue.)"[7]

Sydney Segal, Professor of Pediatrics and Assistant Professor of Obstetrics and Gynecology and Head of the Division of Maternal, Fetal and Neonatal Medicine with the Faculty of Medicine, U.B.C., writes: "One of the special features of smaller community programs is that a skeletal survey may impose on the child a much greater irradiation dose if a community hospital is not equipped with the electronic image intensification apparatus that may be restricted to the most sophisticated pediatric radiology departments."[8]

Subdural hematoma is one of the commonest features of the Battered Child Syndrome, yet by no means all the patients so affected have external marks of injury on the head. This suggests that in some cases repeated acceleration/deceleration rather than direct violence is the cause of the hemorrhage, the infant having been shaken rather than struck by its parent. Such an hypothesis might also explain the remarkable frequency of the finding of subdural hemorrhage in battered children as compared with its incidence in head injuries of other origin.[9]

Infants found mysteriously dead in bed may also be victims of self-induced "whiplash" or abuse. This clue in the age-old puzzle of sudden crib deaths was developed by Abraham Towbin of Boston University School of Medicine. He found hemorrhaging in the spinal column at the neck region in eight of nine such infants examined in autopsies. The hemorrhage indicated to him a snap-injury had occurred to the spinal cord, followed by a suppression of the spinal cord's nerve function. This can happen to a baby put to bed in an apparently healthy condition the night before. Children who are emotionally deprived commonly rock themselves in a very violent fashion.

Towbin points out that an infant's head is large and heavy, making up about a fourth of the body weight. "Structurally," he explains, "the young infant is top heavy. The head is four times as heavy as an adult head in proportion to weight." The heavy head, pivoting atop the unstable spine, leaves the infant vulnerable to self-injury.[10]

John Caffey, writing in "On the Theory and Practice of Shaking Infants— Its Potential Residual Effects of Permanent Brain Damage and Mental Retardation," states: "There is considerable evidence that whiplash-shaking and jolting of infantile heads may be major, unrecognized causes of permanent brain damage and mental retardation. The wide practice of habitual whiplash-shaking for trivial reasons *warrants a massive nation-wide educational campaign* to alert everyone responsible for the welfare of infants on its potential and actual pathogenicity."[11]

In addition, Caffey points out that "potentially dangerous whiplash-shaking is commonly practised under many circumstances, by all kinds of persons, for a wide variety of reasons. The most common motive for repeated whiplash-shaking is to correct minor misbehavior. Such shakings are generally considered innocuous by both parents and physicians. . . . The prevention of such shaking and jerking might substantially reduce the incidence of brain damage and mental retardation."[12]

Consultation with a hematologist is essential in all instances of severe bruising. It is important for both medical and legal reasons to rule out the possibility that the child may have a bleeding disorder, particularly as parents often insist that the child bruises easily, a condition which, in fact, is extremely rare.[13]

Interdisciplinary professionals should particularly note the presence of bruises *on both sides* of the child's face as well as bruises on the back and on the back of the legs. These are good indicators of non-accidental physical abuse.

Robert Bates, Director of the Child Abuse Program within the Department of Pediatrics at The Hospital for Sick Children in Toronto, writes: "Bruising incurred under the guise of acceptable discipline cannot be considered reasonable and safe punishment. Many injuries, such as finger and palm marks on the face or buttocks, speak for themselves, as do human bite marks. Loop and lash marks on the skin are easily identified and indicative of a doubled over cord or belt. Most true accidents cause bruising on only one surface, except when a fall down a stair occurs. In these cases abrasions on the elbows, knees and shoulders would also be expected. Impersonators (the child with a bleeding disorder or a mongolian spot) must not be mistakenly diagnosed as child abuse."[14]

H. Beatty Cotnam, Chief Coroner for the Province of Ontario, specifically referring to bruising, writes: "The Battered Child Syndrome must be considered in any child showing one or more of the following: (1) Multiple bruises of the skin, particularly if they are widespread and of different ages. (2)

Bruising of both sides of the face, on the back of the legs or back."[15]

Cases of child abuse in which bruises are the only physical injuries can be difficult to handle. It is important, therefore, that the physician make use of photography. Colour slides are very helpful in documenting findings of child abuse. However, sometimes colour photos are not admissible in court. Therefore, black and white slides should also be taken.

Segal writes:

> An important source of problems in providing evidence is the photography of a laceration, scald or bruise. In some hospitals there appears to be no problem, but colour photography is prohibited in others. In still others, parental consent must be obtained. In at least one instance, the doctor has a Polaroid camera and can act, therefore, independently of the professional photographers who are becoming increasingly concerned over this question of consent. Perhaps it will be more important to recognize that there could be some legal technicalities associated with Polaroid pictures, as well as any that are developed by someone other than the photographer who may have to prove a continuity, one that could not have allowed for substitution of film. Thus, the use of a police photographer may be preferable. The police photographer would be acting as an agent of a superintendent of child welfare, rather than an investigator in the criminal justice system. The special advantage of police photographers is their competence to use methods incorporating all the legal technicalities that will ensure against the photographs being declared inadmissible in court.[16]

Physicians, hospitals, and police should understand the necessity to photograph correctly child abuse victims because "the quality of the photographs themselves will make or break their admissibility as evidence ... "[17] For a fuller discussion of this subject, see "Photography of Suspected Child Abuse and Maltreatment" by Robert J. Ford, Brian S. Smistek, and James T. Glass in *Biomedical Communications*.[18]

Helfer states that many hospitals are unwilling to photograph a child without parental or court permission, but he states that he has not found it difficult to obtain parental permission if the case has been handled properly. He also points out that, if there is sufficient evidence, court permission can be obtained reasonably quickly. However, in view of the frequency of battering cases, it would be more appropriate to include a "permission to photograph" form among the standard forms filled out by all parents upon admitting children to the hospital.

After all the information and tests have been conducted and assessed, the physician can often make a definite diagnosis.

Should the evidence indicate that the diagnosis is a battered child, the physician must report this to the appropriate agency.

It is essential that the doctor keep accurate records while the child is in his care. If a member of the house staff has taken the initial history and performed the physical examination, the physician should repeat this and countersign the resident's notes. This is extremely important in court procedures where everything not signed by a doctor may be considered hearsay evidence. To avoid this the physician should countersign or write all important notes himself. It is also essential that the doctor state clearly and definitely his findings and opinions, and state that the findings are due to unexplained but *definite trauma*. If the doctor hedges, the child may be returned to the home prematurely, as defence lawyers constantly propose hypothetical situations and ask doctors to state whether or not a child could have been injured in this particular manner. The doctor must continue to remind the court that the situation proposed by the defence lawyer could not happen according to the available medical history. In 25 to 30 per cent of the cases where children have been returned to the home prematurely, abuse recurs.[19]

In a brief submitted to the Standing Committee on Health, Welfare and Social Affairs, Joe Jacobs, Chairman of the Mental Health Committee of the Canadian Paediatric Society, noted that: "The Massachusetts Society for the Prevention of Cruelty to Children found that only nine per cent of willfully injured children were referred by physicians."[20]

Jacobs points out that because we sanction corporal punishment "Family physicians must have a difficult decision to make. The problem in reporting seems to often revolve around at what point does discipline and a parent's rights stop and the welfare of the child begin?"[21]

In the H.A.I.S. report[22] (Home Accident and Injuries Study), the authors point out that 25 per cent of doctors would not report a suspected case to the authorities, while half the physicians[23] then in 1967 did not know the correct reporting procedure. In their own preliminary assessment of cases reported, they felt that the numbers of cases in Canada were much less than in the United States. This was realized to be incorrect but despite setting up a clear list of indications for screening of patients (physical ill treatment, dehydration/malnutrition, neglect, repeated injury, unusually fearful, home accident, burn, scald, poisoning) and guidelines in terms of behaviour of the parents, in two hospitals objections to the project were such that hospital representatives decided not to continue the project.

The reasons given:

    (a) We never see abuse in our hospital.
    (b) This will violate the doctor-patient confidential relationship.
    (c) We don't want to scare away families who need our help.
    (d) We don't have enough staff for this.
    (e) The social agencies don't even know what to do with the cases we find.[24]

Legal protection for the child and the parent is essential, but before legal help can be offered the abuse of the child must be reported to child welfare authorities. Ever since the Battered Child Syndrome and child abuse were first recognized, it has been apparent that protection for the child could best come through early recognition and treatment. This often hinges directly upon the physician's reporting and his willingness to support his diagnosis by medical testimony in court.[25]

A serious difficulty arising in abuse proceedings has been the question of confidential communication between physicians and parents, and in some cases between psychiatrists or social workers and parents. Most physicians in Canada erroneously believe that a privilege of confidentiality exists. In fact, only a lawyer has this privilege. Roman N. Komar, Law Clerk to the Chief Judge, Provincial Courts (Family Division), Brampton, Ontario, notes that one Ontario judge of the Provincial Court (Family Division) felt that even judges and lawyers had to report (despite the recognized solicitor-client privilege) any case of abuse which came to their attention.[26]*

*In Canada, in certain juvenile delinquency matters and in criminal child abuse, the spousal privilege has also been abolished.[27] A federal statute cannot dictate the rules of evidence for a hearing held under a provincial child protection statute. To achieve this protection for the child, each province and territory would have to amend its evidence statute. This amendment, however, would clearly be in the best interests of the child.

An amendment to the Canada Evidence Act to render a spouse compellable as a witness for the prosecution in a child abuse case, subject to judicial discretion, or at least competent to testify at the spouse's own choice,[28] would achieve on an ad hoc or narrow basis what has been proposed on a broad or universal front in the United States,[29] and strongly recommended in Canada. A Study Paper presented in August 1972 by the Law of Evidence Project to the Law Reform Commission of Canada recommended "making the spouse of an accused both competent for and compellable by the Crown as well as the defence in all cases."[30]

Quebec is the only Canadian jurisdiction to have enacted legislation altering the common law to allow testifying physicians in Quebec, if they so wish, to refuse to answer on the basis of professional privilege, unless the patient authorizes the physician to reveal the facts in which case the physician must do so.[31]

Aside from Quebec, "physicians are compellable witnesses on subpoena in Canada and may be required to produce their own records or hospital records that they have in their possession or under their control. In the witness box a physician may not refuse on grounds of professional privilege (unless a statute specifically so provides) to answer a question on matters concerning the patient that are regarded by the court as relevant to the case. The common law position is that the moral and legal duty on the physician to respect the confidences of the patient must give way to the interests of justice in arriving at the truth of the situation."[32]

Unfortunately, the belief in physician-patient confidentiality has often worked to the detriment of the child or the child protection agency. Physicians often assume that the parent is the patient rather than the child, and have protected the parent-physician relationship rather than the child-physician relationship. The physician's duty should be to protect the patient, i.e. the child. Therefore, the principle of privileged communication should be no basis for the reluctance of physicians to testify in child abuse proceedings.[33]

However, more important is the fact that many physicians feel that reporting physically abused children to child welfare authorities is "meddling" or, as has been said, a violation of a professional confidence. In the United States and Canada physicians, though morally and legally urged to report, are not currently fulfilling their function. Many doctors still say they are not prepared to report unless they are guaranteed complete legal immunity. In all provinces where there is a provincial obligation to report, there is a corresponding offer of immunity to the informant. Only the Northwest Territories and Prince Edward Island offer no such immunity, nor do they impose any obligation to report.

It has also been pointed out that doctors are asking for something that is virtually impossible, because all citizens are liable to civil suits even though those actions may be unfounded.[34] Another argument used in defence of non-reporting is the assertion that if physicians did report, parents would become fearful of prosecution and would refuse to take their children to physicians. This has not been borne out where physicians are required to report, and where child abuse registries are maintained.[35] The Committee on the Infant and Pre-School Child of the American Academy of Pediatrics, in supporting mandatory reporting laws, stated that: "The widespread dissemination of the fact that the physician is legally mandated to report a case of suspected child abuse should also remove, or at least reduce, the parent's resentment."[36]

As in the United States, Canadian hospitals and medical boards reflect the doctor's confusion over confidentiality. The result is that police, social workers or solicitors may be refused access to medical records in cases of abused children. Canadian legislative reporting requirements should be designed to overcome not only this inaction, but also the reluctance of physicians to report and become involved in proceedings that end in court and require their appearance as witnesses.

Physicians in Alberta,[37] British Columbia,[38] Manitoba,[39] Newfoundland,[40] Nova Scotia,[41] Ontario,[42] Quebec,[43] Saskatchewan,[44] and The Yukon[45] are required by law to report cases of child abuse to designated authorities. There are differences in the statutory language used in the reporting provisions of these nine jurisdictions, but several generalizations can be made. First, the objective of these reporting provisions is the identification of victims of abuse, or potential victims, so that the resources of the state may be used to protect and assist the child. Second, none of the jurisdictions places special reporting duties on physicians. All nine jurisdictions require "every person" or "any person" having certain information to report. Physicians must report because they are obviously in the class of "every" or "any person." Third, reporting in all nine jurisdictions is mandatory, not merely permissible at the discretion of the physician. In fact, the statutes of all but Saskatchewan specifically provide that the report is required notwithstanding that the information is privileged or confidential. As a result, the physician's ethical and legal duty of professional confidence is displaced in these nine jurisdictions by the statutory duty to make a report.[46]

In the past physicians have feared liability suits as a result of reporting. They may be better advised to fear litigation for failure to report. *The Medical World News,* April 27th, 1973, stated:

> A recent study found that in New York City alone there has been some 23,000 identifiable cases of child battery in a single year. Only eight had been reported by physicians. In many parts of the country the physician must report to the authorities any case of suspected child abuse. Yet even where the law specifically exempts them from liability for erroneous reports, the doctor seldom complies with such a statute.
>
> By failing to report the incident, the doctor usually incurs a misdemeanor penalty. But this may not be the full extent of liability.

The California Penal Code (§11161.5) requires physicians or hospital personnel to report cases of child battery. A suit was filed against four doctors and the police chief of the city of Arroyo Grande alleging that the defendants knew that the child had been battered on several occasions and that they had failed to file reports as required, which would have protected the child from further injury.[47] The case was settled for $900,000 just as the jury was being selected. Apparently counsel for the defendants felt that failure to comply with the statutory reporting requirement created a presumption of negligence.[48]

It should be noted that the Ontario Ministry of Community and Social Services, Children's Services Division, in their *Consultation Paper on Short Term Legislative Amendments* released in December 1977, supported the recommendation made in the 1972 edition of *The Battered Child in Canada* regarding a penalty for physicians and other professionals failing to report suspected child abuse. The Ontario *Consultation Paper* recommends a maximum fine of $1,000 for failure of a professional to report suspected abuse.

TYPICAL CASE PROFILE

AGE	four months
SEX	female
ASSAILANT	father
RECENT EXTERNAL INJURIES	superficial bruise of scalp
FRACTURES	none
INTERNAL INJURIES	contusions, brain; subdural hemorrhage
CAUSE OF DEATH	subdural hemorrhage
PRESENTING STORY	"found in crib, choking"
METHOD OF INJURY	banged baby's head against crib while shaking
REASON FOR INJURY	baby was fussy

CHAPTER 8
Reporting Laws

Plato thought that nature had made some to command, others to serve.[1] He thought the soul of a slave base, incapable of good, unworthy of confidence.[2] Aristotle thought that every well-appointed house needed animate and inanimate tools. The animate tools were slaves, who have souls, but not like those of their masters. Slaves and children lacked will. Slaves and children were like members of the master, ruled by his will. The virtue of children and slaves was obedience.[3]

Roman law gave systematic and enduring form to the rights of masters and slaves. Roman jurists quite openly acknowledged that slaves and children were both persons and things.

The Christian cultural heritage has maintained parental dominance over children. *The New English Bible* states:

> Whoever strikes his father or mother shall be put to death....
> Whoever reviles his father or mother shall be put to death.[4]

Early legislation in North America was clearly for the protection of the parent or the society and not for the benefit of the child. The family was viewed as an institution of social control, and statutory protection of parental (particularly paternal) authority was seen as a necessary tool for preventing children from becoming criminals. The first so-called "stubborn child statute" in Massachusetts, for example, enacted in the 1670s, provided that a stubborn or rebellious son over the age of fifteen years could be put to death on complaint of his parents.[5]

In North American civil law, it has been a well-established principle that a child could not sue its parents in tort* for excessive or brutal punishment. The criminal law provided little protection to children from parental cruelty in that criminal proceedings were only infrequently initiated against parents, and when they were, the courts generally adhered to a presumption in favour of the reasonableness of parental action.[6]

Legal emphasis was not on protecting children for their own sakes but on preventing them from entering into a life of crime and thereby becoming a threat to or drain on society. Neglected, dependent, and delinquent children were all grouped together:[7] "The abject, the vagrant, the delinquent, the child of poverty-stricken or intemperate parents were all proper candidates for one or another asylum or refuge."[8]

Attitudes within the community regarding the rights of ownership over children are still such that the community is loath to interfere in the assault by a parent on a child, even when a similar assault made by one individual upon another would elicit from the community and from the law the response that no citizen has the right to assault another. Biblical sanction has been given to corporal punishment as a means to moral improvement: "Withhold not correction from a child: for if thou strike him with the rod, he shall not die. Thou shalt beat him with the rod, and deliver his soul from hell."[9]

Physical abuse of children is often an indication of a prevailing pattern of caretaker-child interaction in a given home rather than being an isolated incident. Probably more than fifty per cent of abused children have been physically abused prior to the incident that brings them to attention.[10,11]

Richard Gelles, in the United States, found that three of every one hundred parents, an estimated 1.2 million parents countrywide (U.S.), have used knives and guns on their chil-

*Tort is defined as a civil wrong, not including a breach of contract, for which the injured party is entitled to compensation (The Random House College Dictionary, Revised Edition, 1975).

dren. Another 1.2 million have threatened to harm their children with these weapons. The survey indicated that from 3.2 million to 3.9 million children between the ages of three and seventeen have been kicked, bitten, or punched by their parents, and an additional 1.6 million to 2.2 million have been "beaten up" during childhood.[12]

No Canadian figures are available, but there is no reason to believe that the above statistics do not indicate the general North American pattern of parent-child interaction. Although all authorities agree that present reporting of child abuse does not reflect its true incidence, child abuse resulting in murder is ranked as the fifth largest cause of death of American children.[13] It is quite reasonable to believe that these figures also reflect the situation in Canada.

The number of children who die as a result of accidents should also be examined because they include a large number of incorrectly diagnosed deaths. In addition, suicide statistics, as high as they are among adolescents, only reflect a portion of the suicides of children, and indeed often of very young children, whose deaths have been suicides diagnosed as accidents.[14]

The recent recognition by experts in the field of learning disorders[15] regarding the number of children who suffer gross to minimal learning dysfunction must also be examined from the assumption that a certain number of these children were victims of assault or physical or emotional neglect. Add to this the high incidence of mental illness that could be attributed to emotional abuse, and a truer picture of the care and treatment costs for victims of child abuse might be estimated.

In the first annual report of the Quebec Youth Protection Committee, covering the first eighteen months of operation from October 1st, 1975 to March 31st, 1977, 3,102 reports of child abuse were verified and evaluated.[16] The Youth Protection Committee believes that each year about five per cent of these children die of their injuries, while over forty per cent suffer physical or psychological effects for the rest of their lives.[17] Translated into legal terms, this means that there were 155 murders or manslaughters and 1,240 gross assaults resulting in a high risk of permanent disability in Quebec alone in the period October 1st, 1975 to March 31st, 1977. Until most recently, death at the hands of one's parents was not treated, classified, or in most cases even thought of in terms of murder.

Provincial registries were set up to protect children. They were designed to acquaint medical, legal, and social service personnel with the fact that a particular child was considered at risk. If a suspected case of child abuse came to the attention of personnel, by checking with the registry they could support their diagnosis.

Instituted in early 1974, the Alberta Child Protection Registry, for instance, maintains a record of all reports of child abuse, particularly where child battering is confirmed or suspected. The reports are screened by the registry supervisor who directs the necessary follow-up measures.[18]*

Injuries to children are often passed off as "accidental." Although accidental injuries are relatively common in children, recent statistics have shown that approximately 18 per cent of the child injury cases reported as accidents were not accidental.[19]

Child protection registries are set up to provide a centralized record of battery cases. Once reported, individuals implicated in child battering cannot remain undetected by moving from community to community, or by seeking medical aid from various doctors and hospitals.[20]

The Child Welfare Act of Alberta (1973, c. 15, s. 8) states as follows:

41. (1) Any person who has reasonable and probable ground to believe that a child has been abandoned, deserted, physically ill-treated or is in need of protection shall report the ground of such belief to the Director or to any child welfare worker of the Department.

(2) Subsection (1) applies notwithstanding that the ground for belief is information that is confidential or privileged, and no action lies against the person so reporting unless the provision of the report is done maliciously or without reasonable and probable ground for belief.

(3) Any person who fails to comply with subsection (1), in addition to any civil liability, is guilty of an offence and liable upon summary conviction to a fine of not more than $500 and in default of payment to imprisonment for a term not exceeding six months or to both fine and imprisonment.†

41.1 The Director shall maintain a registry for the purpose of recording all reports received under section 41.

41.2 Upon a report being made pursuant to section 41, the Director shall

---

Nova Scotia has also provided for such a register by legislation.[21] Other provinces have them too, but more by administrative directive than by statute.

†Although enacted in 1973, subsection (3), as of 1978, had not yet been proclaimed in force.

cause the report to be examined and shall direct such further investigations of the matter reported as he considers necessary.

Alberta's child abuse legislation is representative of most provincial laws. However, only the Yukon Territory provides a specific penalty for failure to report *in its reporting provision*.[22] The jurisdictions of British Columbia, Manitoba, Newfoundland, Nova Scotia, Quebec, and Saskatchewan impose a penalty for failure to report either in their reporting provisions or through their various summary convictions legislation.[23] New Brunswick, the Northwest Territories, and Prince Edward Island impose no obligation to report. However, the New Brunswick legislation grants civil immunity to any informant.[24] Alberta's penalty section has not yet been proclaimed in force and Ontario imposes only a bare obligation to report.[25]

In Canada there are many family courts. They go by different names; in Ontario, they are called provincial courts (family division); in Manitoba, the provincial judges' courts (family division). In Alberta, on the other hand, there is a unitary court structure, one family court for the entire province, even though it may sit and have courtrooms all over the province.

Family courts were created at different times by the various provinces. It is true that in Ottawa and Toronto, certain police magistrates in the 1920s were scheduled to hear nothing but domestic, juvenile, and child protection cases. But this was purely an internal administrative arrangement. They were still police magistrates' courts, not "family courts." Saskatchewan and Prince Edward Island were latecomers; but then neither the Northwest Territories nor the Yukon Territory have any family courts as yet. There, child protection matters are still handled by magistrates sitting as a "juvenile court."

"Juvenile courts" handled child protection matters prior to the creation of the family courts. Prior to the juvenile courts, a magistrate's court or a justice of the peace dealt with neglected children.

In respect of children, these courts exercised a certain measure of *parens patriae* powers – a body of rules developed by the English Court of Chancery for the judicial supervision of the obligations owed by guardians to their wards.

It was assumed that these courts would protect the child. The manner in which its proceedings were conducted were determined largely by the individual presiding judge.[26] The proponents of the system saw little need for adherence to rules of procedure designed to protect the rights of persons appearing before other tribunals. During its early years, fault was found by some because the informality of the family court did not go far enough. By design and by default, legal safeguards available to litigants appearing before other courts were sometimes denied to parties in family court proceedings.[27]

Given the present climate of concern for the rights of individuals, it is not surprising that attention is being directed toward the family court. Legal services available through Human Rights and Civil Liberties Associations and Legal Aid have brought the lawyer more frequently into the family court. In some cases what they saw shocked their sense of fair play.[28]

The discussion of the family courts has shifted, therefore, from the earlier criticism about lack of informality, to criticism over the lack of formality. What once was considered an undue emphasis upon legal rights has shifted to complaints about the inadequacy of such safeguards. It is suggested that the delicate balance between the social aspects of the court and the legal principles that should guide it have been overweighted on the side of informality of procedure with resulting injustice and violations of legal rights.[29]

Family courts, with their informal hearings, are also, in some provinces, presided over by magistrates who, outside of the larger cities, may be laymen. In these situations an unofficial hierarchy of witnesses may strongly influence the way in which these cases are conducted.[30]

Each province has legislation for the protection of the child outlining neglect and physical abuse, etc., as causes for provincial intervention. Within the jurisdiction of these provincial laws, however, there is a wide range of interpretations in the minds of child-care workers, magistrates, and the community as to what constitutes abuse. To complicate an already complicated situation, there is the question of emotional abuse. Mental health workers are able to give substantial evidence to the effect that emotional abuse can be measured in physical terms. For instance, deprivation of love may result in symptoms of retardation.[31,32] The law, however, is not yet capable of defining emotional abuse or neglect with any certainty.

When persons are involved in child protection proceedings, as in other litigation, they seek recognition or enforcement of their rights. A person shall not be deprived of liberty, property, the custody of a child or the right to parental care without "due process of law." The due process of law, however, is not an absolute in all cases. The right of litigants may vary considerably according to the purpose of the litigation. A person who causes serious physical injury to another person may be prosecuted in the criminal court for the crime of assault. Guilt, however, must be proved by evidence that establishes beyond reasonable doubt every element of the crime charged. If sued by an injured party in a civil court for damages that involve money, only a preponderance of evidence is sufficient to establish liability.[33]

Child abuse protective proceedings are deemed civil, and the rights of the parties are primarily governed by the rules that apply in other civil proceedings. The parent does not have the right to demand that the abuse of the child be proven beyond every reasonable doubt. However, the child has the right to the protection of the law if abuse is established by a preponderance of evidence. Because most child abuse incidents take place without witnesses, it is often very hard to prove beyond a reasonable doubt that this or that individual perpetrated this or that assault.[34] The child should not be deprived of protection because evidence falls short of the reasonable doubt test.

The intent of these hearings is to establish the safety or lack of safety of the child's environment, based on questions of the ability of the parents to provide a safe environment, rather than on the guilt or innocence of the parents.

Borrowing the principle *res ipsa loquitur* from the evidentiary law of negligence has allowed American and Canadian judges in child abuse proceedings to set precedents for accepting the proposition that the condition of the child speaks for itself. The Latin term *res ipsa loquitur* states "the thing speaks for itself," meaning that the instrument which caused the damage was so much under the defendant's control that the injury could only be attributable to or explicable in terms of negligence. This act of negligence "speaks for itself."

The use of this proposition permits an inference of neglect to be drawn from proof of the child's age and condition, and that in the ordinary course of child-rearing such a condition does not occur if the parent who has the responsibility and control of a child is protective and non-abusive.[35]

Although the freedom and relaxed atmosphere of the family court is in many ways good, records of proceedings kept in these courts and reports and documents tendered into evidence at trial, unlike those in criminal and other civil court actions, are generally treated as confidential.

Because child abuse is not regarded as a crime, the reputation of the victim is not considered to be as important as the reputation of the parents. Therefore, confidentiality has worked to the detriment of the child.

In the past, the only records available for study and evidence were from the occasional case that had been appealed. Regular case hearings were not available. Therefore, no case law could be built for the guidance of future hearings.[36]*

Increasingly, judges are handing down written reasons for judgment, and some of these are regularly reported in the *Reports of Family Law*. Komar notes that, most often, the reasons for judgment are given orally (simply because the case turns on a simple finding of fact, rather than any question of law). Oral reasons are recorded on the "record" of the Court, but no transcript is ever made. Komar suggests that simple lack of interest may account for this.

It is not acceptable or appropriate that each protective child care worker or even each magistrate or judge set his or her own standards. The question before the law is what are the minimum standards of child care.[37] Obviously these standards must be understood and accepted before any realistic approach to the complicated question of the rights of the child is possible.

In whatever way these standards are modified, however, due process in child protective proceedings does require that all parties in each adjudication be treated the same. Parents in abuse cases should be given proper notice sufficiently in advance of their hearing to permit preparation. Notice should also be sufficiently specific to tell the respondent what is involved so that he or she can choose intelligently whether to acquiesce or contest, and to know what to refute if he or she decides to contest. If, however, it has been impossible to locate the parent, the court may proceed with the hearings.

Another area of concern involves testimony. To testify in a courtroom and to be cross-examined is not easy or pleasant. It can be additionally difficult for parents, children, and chil-

---

Komar notes that all family courts in Canada are "courts of record." That means that a stenographer or an electronic recorder is used to gather up every word spoken in Court.

dren's aid or social service workers on child protective cases. For instance, child abuse workers who understand the difficulties faced by the child and the necessity to protect the child are often nevertheless loath to upset the relationship they may have established with the parents. In some cases parents have been excluded from the courtroom during the presentation of the petitioner's case on the grounds that to allow the parents to hear the petitioner's testimony would damage the case worker-parent relationship or the parent-child relationship. Whether the procedures are tightened or relaxed, they cannot be made to order to fit individual cases. The requirements of "due process of law" in family courts should be uniform across Canada.

The *Criminal Code* of Canada contains numerous provisions related to the abused, neglected, or sexually assaulted child.

Sec. 168(1) states:

> Everyone who, in the home of a child, participates in adultery or sexual immorality or indulges in habitual drunkenness or any other form of vice, and thereby endangers the morals of the child or renders the home an unfit place for the child to be in, is guilty of an indictable offence and is liable to imprisonment for two years.[38]

Sec. 197(1) states:

> Everyone is under a legal duty (a) as a parent, foster parent, guardian or head of a family, to provide necessaries of life for a child under the age of sixteen years.[39]

Sec. 200 states:

> Everyone who unlawfully abandons or exposes a child who is under the age of ten years, so that its life is or is likely to be endangered or its health is or is likely to be permanently injured, is guilty of an indictable offence and is liable to imprisonment for two years.[40]

Other offences do not distinguish between a child or adult but apply equally. These are described under a number of headings from Assault to Murder.

Sec. 204 states:

> Everyone who by criminal negligence causes bodily harm to another person is guilty of an indictable offence and is liable to imprisonment for ten years.[41]

Sec. 205(1) states:

> A person commits homicide when, directly or indirectly, by any means, he causes the death of a human being.[42]

Murder, manslaughter, and infanticide, Sections 212, 217,

and 216 respectively, are all charges that can be related to the death of a child where abuse is suspected.[43]

Occasionally children are administered noxious substances. Sec. 229 states:

> Everyone who administers or causes to be administered to any person or causes any person to take poison or any other destructive or noxious thing is guilty of an indictable offence and is liable (a) to imprisonment for fourteen years, if he intends thereby to endanger the life of or to cause bodily harm to that person; or (b) to imprisonment for two years, if he intends thereby to aggrieve or annoy that person.[44]

Various forms of assault, whether it be physical or sexual assault, are described within the *Criminal Code*. Although in the past these charges have been laid primarily in cases of adults assaulting adults, they apply equally to children.

Sexual abuse offences against children are covered in the *Criminal Code* by Section 146(1), Sexual Intercourse with Female between 14-16 Years of Age; Section 166, Parent or Guardian Procuring Intercourse with Child; Section 149, Indecent Assault of Female Person; Section 150, Incest; Section 151, Seduction of Female between 16-18 Years of Age; Section 153(1)(a), Sexual Intercourse with Stepdaughter, Foster Daughter, or Female Ward; Section 155, Buggery; Section 156, Indecent Assault on Male; and Section 157, Acts of Gross Indecency.

Sexual abuse of children, for instance, is rarely reported, or is reported only after it has gone on for a long period of time, even though the abuse was known to the rest of the family. Wives commonly do not report because of shame and/or embarrassment, or because of fear and/or threats. Wives have been beaten to discourage such reporting. Also, the wife fears that reporting will endanger the family's financial security and eventually result in the break-up of the family unit. She is often convinced that the husband's actions towards the child will cease if given time.[45]

In almost all cases the victimized is a girl. The median age for child victims is twelve years.[46] The numbers of young girls who become alcoholic, runaways, suicidal, or promiscuous has yet to be studied in terms of home environments in which incest is a factor.[47]

A child is a "person" in Canadian law, but like an individual who is insane, is under certain legal disabilities. A child or an insane person is not regarded in law as capable of managing his or her own affairs. Parents are natural guardians, but can be replaced by a court-appointed guardian. The reason why children have so few visible rights is the same as why people in mental institutions have few rights. In theory, they have all the rights of other persons; the problem is how to get their guardians to enforce them.

Justice William O. Douglas, before his retirement, eloquently commented on the numbers of American children incarcerated on the whim of their parents simply because they do not obey their parents' commands.[48] In addition, Allan Berman and Andrew Siegal, writing in "A Neuropsychological Approach to the Etiology, Prevention, and Treatment of Juvenile Delinquency," note that more than seventy per cent of youngsters are initially confined to a training school for a relatively minor offence such as truancy or running away from home.[49]

The B.C. Royal Commission on Family and Children's Law states: "A reason for introducing the legal rights of children arises from the existing legal position of the child in our system of justice. In a word, the child's legal position is non-existent."[50]

TYPICAL CASE PROFILE

AGE	eighteen months
SEX	female
ASSAILANT	sibling
RECENT EXTERNAL INJURIES	thermal burns, lower trunk and lower extremities
FRACTURES	none
CAUSE OF DEATH	shock with thermal burns, unattended
PRESENTING STORY	"placed baby's bottom in hot water, then fell and dropped baby in overturned water"
METHOD OF INJURY	same as indicated
REASON FOR INJURY	baby soiled floor

CHAPTER 9
The Social Worker's Dilemma

From numerous interviews with social workers who work at the community level, it becomes disturbingly clear that child abuse is an increasingly important part of their work in Canada. Social service agencies play the central role in identifying, helping, and protecting battered, neglected, and abused children. It is to these agencies that referrals and reports of abused children are made. If a case has been dealt with by the courts, it is often the agency's responsibility to maintain contact with the case, attempt to offer continued protection for the child, and provide further assistance to the family.

Agency referrals often come from officers of health and public health nurses. Doctors and hospitals account for a small percentage of referrals. Some reports come from police, some from neighbours and relatives, and some from the occasional school teacher.

In one case a child who was already in the hospital was reported by a teacher. In making the report the teacher said that this child had been severely bruised on several other occasions, but that her principal had advised her to "stay out of the situation." But this further episode, which had resulted in a fractured skull, had been "too much for her" and she had reported it to a social agency.[1] Had the teacher not made this report, it is fairly certain that the attending physician would have treated the skull fracture and released the child back to the parents without any investigation.

In interview after interview, social workers asserted that, almost without exception, they were unable to secure the supporting testimony of physicians in cases of child battering. They complained bitterly that physicians refused to write medical histories clearly stating that, in their opinion, a child had suffered abuse. Doctors find it easier to say that the injury is unexplained. The theme that emerged from these interviews was consistent. Social workers despair over equivocation and lack of support on the part of physicians. Time and time again they reported that they were unable to get doctors to appear in court, and that doctors actually refused to become involved. Unless the physician is willing to state that the child is severely injured and should not be discharged from the hospital to the home, and unless he is willing to support this in court, the welfare or law enforcement agency is usually unable to pursue the case with any degree of authority.[2,3]

Without statistics, social workers are unable to convince physicians that child battering is a factor of Canadian life and that this is the cause of death for many children. Yet because the statistics are so completely linked to the doctor and to the doctor's reporting, social agencies are unable to present an accurate picture of child battering. It is interesting that, until recently, statistically the battered child in Canada hardly existed. The battered child disappeared under other categories or was ignored completely, thereby leaving hospitals, physicians and even upper echelons in government departments free to assure the investigator that very few battered children existed.

Without physicians', coroners' and medical examiners' reports, proper statistics can never be available. The record of physicians with regard to the question of child abuse is so embarrassingly bad that it is almost painful to dwell on it. It suffices to say that, so far as the Battered Child Syndrome is concerned, physicians stand completely indicted.

The battered child is abandoned not only by the physicians and the hospitals, but often by the law and judicial bodies as well.* Another common complaint of social workers and social service people is that once cases of abuse are brought before the courts, they are often heard before insensitive magistrates who lack understanding of the Battered Child Syndrome. As a result they often make casual assessments of these cases and recommend that the child be returned to the home. Many magistrates feel that they can deal with the problems of an abused child by ordering that a social worker make regular visits to the home, unaware that the case load of the social agency is such that "regular visits" turn out in practice to be a half-hour visit once a month.

Social workers are in close agreement with Dr. C. H. Kempe, who writes:

> Case work alone (that is the visits of a social worker into the family) is apt to be a dangerous method of handling the problem, and protective services should be extremely cautious about assuming the responsibility for leaving the injured child in the home, especially if the child has been badly battered and is under three years of age.[4]

Another complaint which social workers make is that often children who have been removed from the home are returned prematurely to the parents by the magistrate or judge. Dr. Kempe explains:

> This is almost invariably a dangerous procedure which frequently leads to repeated injury and is often fatal. In our experience errors have been made primarily in the direction of leaving the child in the home under the supervision of case workers in protective services and then experiencing a second and third series of injuries or death.[5,6]

In other words, social workers bear out Dr. Kempe's feeling that while the intentions of the court are good, judges and magistrates often recommend supervision which the departments responsible cannot possibly fulfil. The result is that the child is virtually abandoned.

> Often the decision to leave a battered child in his environment is made with the understanding by all concerned that close and continuous supervision will occur and that this will hopefully prevent a repetition of the injury. Careful investigation often reveals that close and continuous supervision does not in fact occur, and that while the welfare department, the police, relatives and others all remain interested, each expects the other to perform this vital role. Further, by simply moving to another county

---

The police are very often quite sensitive and helpful in reporting cases of child battering, but like other social agencies are unable to provide continuing protection for the child.

within the state, families can often become no longer available for supervision and care.*[7]

Social workers also point out that in cases where home visits have only been *recommended* by a magistrate, social workers are in a difficult position because the parents often simply avoid them by failing to keep appointments which they have made.[9] On the other hand, parents may put on a performance when the social worker visits, while at other times they continue their general pattern of abuse and the state of the child is as miserable as ever. Case histories also make it abundantly clear that some social workers have actually failed to see the child and instead have spent the complete visit talking only to the mother, unaware that the child was in a badly damaged state upstairs.[10] Also there are parents who put up a front as if they intend to "graciously comply with the agency's expectations in order to get the case worker out of their lives."[11]

Jean Roberts, Head of Family Services for the Ottawa Children's Aid Society, states in her study entitled *Characteristics of the Abused Child and His Family, An Agency Study*:

> If we subscribe to the idea that doctors must be alert to suspicious circumstances, then we must place some responsibility on social workers for more thorough exploration of events which appear blindly in records and remain obscure because the worker failed to take proper cognizance of them.[12]

A comment on this, however, might be that social workers are often underpaid, burdened with impossible case loads, and receive very little support from the community.

In addition, social workers are often left to acquire their understanding of these cases empirically, and are hence often unprepared, either by the social agencies whom they represent or by their training in the schools of social work, to deal with them.**

At present very few schools of social work in Canada pro-

---

*An agency study in Ottawa states that of seven children who were returned home, the social agency anticipates that six will be subjected to further abuse.[8]

**In July of 1976, Ross Dawson, Assistant Director of the Sault Ste. Marie and District of Algoma Children's Aid Society and Chairman of the subcommittee of the Ontario Association of Children's Aid Societies Services Committee, prepared an excellent set of Guidelines for Practice and Procedure in Handling Cases of Child Abuse for the Ontario Association of Children's Aid Societies.

vide the necessary curriculum to equip social workers to deal with the complicated and specialized area of battered children.*[13]

Further, social workers in Canada find that provincial child protection acts often do not require social agencies to investigate all complaints of suspected child abuse. This situation would automatically be rectified by federal and provincial co-operation in the passing of standardized legislation, with a provision to include mandatory investigation of these cases.

J. V. Belknap, Superintendent of Child Welfare for British Columbia, states:

> We need to build provisions in our statutes whereby a family's situation can be received and reviewed and appropriate services be made available on a mandatory basis with provisions for follow-up review by the court. In instances where circumstances are such that a preponderance of evidence points to neglect or battering, the court should be empowered to order that the parents be evaluated by a medical team and be placed under a regime of medico-socio treatment. The court should be empowered to order in a homemaker or family aides or make necessary, regular contacts by the social worker or public health nurse for counselling, or require the parents to attend a Parents Effectiveness Course much like we do in making the faulty driver take a defensive driving course.[14]

Belknap also speaks of the major problem in delivery services.

> One of the most worrisome aspects of the situation from my point of view is the lack of understanding of roles and functions that exist between professional disciplines and between various agencies and institutions. Accompanying this lack of understanding goes lack of confidence, trust and often outright rivalry. There is often little or no collaboration or commitment to various roles or skill areas existing between the professions.[15]

Many social workers feel bitter about their inability to cope with a problem of this magnitude. Social agencies, unable to rally the support of physicians, all too often face magistrates and defence lawyers for parents who feel that these agencies are out to baby-snatch and wantonly remove children from their rightful parents.

While it is true that mistakes have been made on the part of social agencies in removing children from their homes, it is also true that the major errors have been consistently on the side of returning children to their homes only to find that these children are again abused.[16] It is an old fantasy that the bad

*Canadian schools of social work still do not routinely include the problem of battered, abused, or neglected children as part of their formal curriculum.

Children's Aid Society or social worker wants to destroy a beautiful home simply out of failure to understand the eccentricity of parents in dealing with their children.

The feeling of hopelessness and futility common to many social workers can be exemplified by the worker who took a severely battered child to hospital and was unable to find any physician who would testify that the child was abused. As a result of a lack of medical evidence, the social agency was forced to return this child to the abusive parents only to have the child die within two weeks.[17]

The Minister of Health and Welfare, addressing the Standing Committee on Health, Welfare and Social Affairs on December 16th, 1975, said: "Without prejudice to any individuals or programs, governmental or voluntary, our systems of delivering needed services to children and their families are frequently fragmented, overlapping or lacking in coordination and integration. While this has not prevented the substantial progress which has been made in the child welfare field in the recent past, it remains a matter to which attention must be given as we contemplate future action to protect children and prevent abuse and neglect."[18]

Yude M. Henteleff, Immediate Past President of the Canadian Association for Children with Learning Disabilities,* in his 1976 brief to the Solicitor General of Canada on the proposed federal Act "Young Persons in Conflict with the Law," stated that: "It is our view and shared by many others, that a good many of the care agencies to which many children are now referred are, at their best, worse than the worst kind of parents."[19]

This statement by Henteleff is often corroborated by those individuals and agencies who have examined Canadian child protection services. However, the high incidence of runaway Canadian children substantiates the fact that, for many children, home is intolerable.

Most often there is no place for the abused child to be well-nurtured. If the society wishes to pay in perpetuity for crimes

---

*The Canadian Association for Children With Learning Disabilities is a national organization dedicated to the advancement of the education and general welfare of children and youth who have learning disabilities of a perceptual, conceptual or co-ordinative nature or related problems. These children are of normal or above normal intelligence, general retardation or emotional disturbance not being the causative factors of their problems.

and mental illness, it will continue to fail to provide funding to create appropriate treatment centres and youth housing projects in which children can seek and find not only shelter but good accommodation. It is neither necessary nor appropriate to treat children who have been abused as criminals or second-class citizens. Children whose parents for whatever reasons cannot nurture could be provided with a guaranteed income and pleasant, appropriate physical and emotional accommodations at far less cost than the present cost of incarceration or remedial assistance currently provided by an inadequate and often outright pernicious so-called helping system.

As for the Canadian infant at risk, C. Henry Kempe, in his 1975 Armstrong Lecture, "A Vindication of the Rights of Children," concluded that:

> In a free society the newborn child does not belong to the state, does not belong to the parents, but belongs to himself in the care of the parents. When parenting is defective or blatantly harmful, prompt intervention by society is essential on behalf of the suffering child and also of the suffering parents.
>
> Universal, egalitarian and compulsory health supervision, in the broadest sense of the term, is the right of every North American child. Access to regular health supervision should not be left to the motivation of the parents, but must be guaranteed by society.
>
> Utilization of indigenous health visitors (successful, supportive, mature mothers acceptable to the community) to provide a bridge between the young family and health services is the most inexpensive, least threatening and efficient approach to give the child the greatest possible chance to reach their potential.[20]

AGE	three years
SEX	male
ASSAILANT	father
RECENT EXTERNAL INJURIES	bruises, linear and loop, on face, trunk, and extremities
REMOTE EXTERNAL INJURIES	healed linear scars, lower extremities
FRACTURES	none
INTERNAL INJURIES	severe cerebral edema; cerebral contusion
CAUSE OF DEATH	cerebral contusion
PRESENTING STORY	"fell downstairs"
METHOD OF INJURY	beaten with wire coathanger
REASON FOR INJURY	"strewing contents of cabinet"

CHAPTER 10
The Abused Child in the School System

In 1969, Gil pointed out that schools could be a valuable screening and reporting facility for detecting child abuse, but have been neglected until very recently. He recommended educating teachers in recognition and reporting of abuse.[1]

The following signs should arouse a teacher's suspicion that a child is suffering from physical ill-treatment:

— The child may often be tired.
— The child may be unusually or exceptionally quiet, uncommunicative, fearful of authority and of other children. He or she may wince if touched.
— The child often has bruises or burns not usually associated with play.
— The child may refuse to participate in gym for no valid reason, in an attempt to conceal injuries.
— The child may be frequently absent from school and then appear with fading bruises.

- The child may or may not complain of abuse. Often the child is afraid to tell. When questioned, the child may deny the abuse or give an illogical explanation for an injury.
- The child may be a boy or a girl and may be one of other siblings who are *not* abused.

While abuse is more frequently observed in families of a lower socio-economic group whose way of life is more exposed to the community, it can also occur in

- families who keep a clean house and keep their children well dressed;
- families who attend church and occupy a "respectable" position in the community;
- families who are not hard up or do not have other obvious problems.

What should a teacher do if child abuse is suspected? Call the provincial child protection agency *immediately*. Early reporting is urgent, while an injury is still in evidence. The agency will take the necessary steps to find out if the child is in need of protection.

Such action does not necessarily result in children being removed from their homes. Only if a child is in serious danger will it be removed and then only with due process of law.

Child abuse is not something that happens to just infants and pre-schoolers. Richard Gelles,[2] a University of Rhode Island professor of sociology and anthropology who studies violence in the home, states that: "We've always operated under the assumption that little children were the main targets of parent abuse, but figures indicate there may be a whole new area."

A seventeen-year-old is as likely to be abused by parents as a three-year-old. In a study of 285 freshmen, twenty-six per cent reported that their parents had used some kind of physical violence during their last year at home, ranging from spankings to threats at gunpoint. The study showed that twelve per cent reacted to parent abuse by fighting back, in many cases actually punching a parent. Fifteen per cent of the sample said they saw their parents strike each other in the home. Eight per cent said they were physically injured by their parents during their senior year of high school but, Gelles said, "An even more accurate figure would be ten or twelve per cent." He explained that many college freshmen are probably embarrassed to admit they were abused.

Gelles said ten per cent of the male students and eight per cent of the females reported physical injury and required treatment ranging from a bandaid to hospital emergency room care.[3] No Canadian figures are available, but there is no reason to believe that this is not a North American pattern of parent-child interaction.

Further support for the concept that parental violence spawns juvenile violence came from a study that found that the strongest bond between juvenile delinquents in street gangs was a result of their need for protection from the violent physical and verbal assaults perpetrated on their persons and characters by their parents, primarily their fathers. Repressed and overt violence is the other common denominator, according to a study of 356 delinquent fifteen- to eighteen-year-olds in three Philadelphia correctional institutions by psychologists C. Jack Friedman and Frederica Mann of the Abington Hospital in Abington, Pennsylvania.

The necessity to introduce respect for the law within the home is also reflected in the fact that more than half of all serious crimes in the United States (murder, rape, aggravated assault, robbery, burglary, larceny, motor vehicle theft) are committed by youths.[4]

The child who is bullied in the home bullies in the street. Robins, in *Deviant Children Grown Up*, has shown that the best predictor of sociopathic behaviour in adulthood is sociopathic behaviour in childhood.[5] In other words, the aggressive and bullying child grows up to be the bullying and aggressive adult.

The concept that the parents' home is their castle has provided a structure whereby arbitrary parental authority has superseded the Criminal Code of Canada as well as provincial child protection legislation. This is evidenced not only by the physical abuse of children, but is reflected in the fact that more policemen are killed interfering in domestic disturbances than in almost any other line of duty. Today, many schools have had to resort to the use of security guards for the protection of students and teachers. Teachers are increasingly assaulted and abused.

The crisis of violence in the North American home and school clearly indicates the need for a revamping of the curriculum to provide the child population with, first, a complete understanding of its legal rights to protection. Obviously schools should clearly post, for students and teachers, child protection legislation, as well as a list for teachers and students of support agencies available to students who are abused or at risk. Second is the necessity to create a balanced curriculum of family life education programs to provide the vital information to prevent further abuse. The importance of the school as an institution for preventing the abuse of children is inestimable.

In their August 1976 *Committee Report on the Abused and Battered Child*, the Federation of Women Teachers' Associations of Ontario stated:

> Parenting is the most difficult, the most challenging, the most significant, and the least mastered and most promising frontier.[6]

> Abuse creates abuse. Abused children come to view abuse as an acceptable method of child-rearing and, on becoming parents themselves, use abusive methods in bringing up their own children.[7] Robert Bates, Paediatrician and Director of the Child Abuse Team at the Hospital for Sick Children in Toronto, states that this year (1976) there will be close to 700 child abuse cases in the city of Toronto.

> The abuse cycle can be broken[8] if an attempt can be made to inform potential parents of the philosophies, practicalities and the pitfalls of parenthood. Perhaps society can rid itself of some of the shameful indignities and the physical pain suffered by all too many innocent children.

> In their work with "problem children" the medical profession and social agencies are discovering more and more that the source of many of the difficulties that these children experience is the lack of adequate parenting skills.[9]

> Many professionals involved in the treatment of problem children now believe that the only way to insure better parenting in the coming generations is to offer a course in parenting at all levels in the school system. Here, the greatest number of prospective parents could be influenced. To our knowledge, a course of this type has not yet been developed in Canada.[10]

The necessity to implement the recommendations of the Federation of Women Teachers' Associations of Ontario is a first priority. Unless a curriculum designed to acquaint children with good parenting is created, a bad situation can only worsen. It is urgent that the abused child be intercepted in the school at the earliest point.

The school, however, is much more than just the recipient of children who are abused at home. The school itself stands indicted as an institution that severely abuses children, both emotionally and physically.

Shirley Amiel, writing in "Child Abuse in Schools," notes that 4.5 million children may be exposed to teachers who are maladjusted. Estimates indicate that twenty-five per cent are unhappy, worried, or dissatisfied, seventeen per cent are unusually nervous and nine per cent are judged maladjusted, according to the results of psychological tests.[11]

In a new study of negative behaviour, John M. Branan, inspired by the late Abraham Maslow's statement that the most important area for young psychologists to illuminate was evil or what makes persons behave negatively,[12] asked 150 of his students to write up in detail what they considered the two most negative experiences in their lives – experiences that made their lives worse or that hindered their development. The students related many instances in which teachers had humiliated them in front of a class, evaluated them unfairly, destroyed their self-confidence, or embarrassed them.

Of the 300 experiences they listed, Branan classified 43 as "nonpersonal"; these involved religion (3) and accidents or illnesses (40). The 257 others were "interpersonal" experiences that involved teachers at all grade levels far more often than any other persons, even parents. The numerical breakdown, on the basis of who was involved, was: teachers – 84; parents – 59; friends or acquaintances – 37; boy- or girl-friends – 32; strangers – 28; brothers or sisters – 17.

Branan believes that human-relations training would lessen "the damage resulting from sarcastic, insensitive and noncaring teachers" and should be a prerequisite to getting teacher credentials.[13] Aside from sarcasm and verbal abuse, many teachers hit, pinch, pull, yank, and otherwise assault students.

An April 19th, 1977 United States Supreme Court decision ruled that the American Constitution does not protect children from teachers who wish to use physical force to discipline them. (One of the boys who lost the case was said to have been struck more than twenty times with a paddle for being "slow to respond to his teacher's instructions.") Since the decision, a number of teachers' groups have announced that they are well satisfied with it. "Teachers want corporal punishment retained as an option," said the executive director of the Houston Teachers Association. "No one likes to see [his] options limited." A spokesman for the American Federation of Teachers said, "Teachers want to maintain a healthy atmosphere and they need options."

An editorial in *The New Yorker* states: "'Options' is a neutral-sounding word, but common sense told us that where these teachers were concerned we would not want to be on the receiving end of any exercised options. These teachers were using the word 'options' as a cool synonym for 'weapons'."* The editorial continues:

> In reality, there is no balance of terror between adults and children. There is an emormous imbalance, with adults holding most of the power and children feeling most of the terror. The teachers who want the "option" of physical violence – not for self-defense but to enforce their rules – are talking as if, deprived of paddle technology, deprived even of the use of their bare hands, they could not find any other means of terrorizing children. This is not true. In Detroit, for instance, some of the public schools have been punishing students for "misbehavior" by a method called "dry lunch". The students are not allowed to have hot lunches or any drinks from the school cafeteria; they may bring lunches from home, but no drinks, and neither may they use the drinking fountain.
>
> People talk about child abuse as if it were something sensational and aberrant (vicious beatings, the use of children in pornography), and they idealize "normal" childhood. The Supreme Court's majority opinion in the school-discipline case said that the Eighth Amendment protects prisoners but not school-children from "cruel and unusual punishments", because "the prisoner and the school-child stand in wholly different circumstances, separated by the harsh facts of criminal conviction and incarceration." But childhood, which is marked by systematic humiliations, large and small, is much more like incarceration than it is like a state of autonomous power against which adults must defend themselves and their rules with unlimited "options".[14]

In Canada, Marge Csapo, Professor of Special Education at U.B.C., and Bernie Aag, a Probationary Officer, recently completed a three-year study in Vancouver of hard-core delinquents all on the verge of being transferred to adult court. Their 1976 study showed that school failure was one of the major causative factors of their respective conditions, a cause that has been largely ignored.[15]

Across the board, new data supports the concept that not all children can accept sarcasm, humiliation, and corporal punishment with good cheer. A percentage at least react aggressively, disruptively, or violently. The cost of vandalism in North American schools runs to many millions of dollars. Clearly, vandalism is an expression of hatred toward teachers and not toward buildings.

*The New York Times reported that in Dade County, Florida (where the case that reached the Supreme Court originated), the paddles must be of wood and must not exceed two feet in length, four inches in width, and one-half inch in thickness.

AGE	five years
SEX	male
ASSAILANT	foster parents
RECENT EXTERNAL INJURIES	numerous bruises on scalp, face, and trunk
REMOTE EXTERNAL INJURIES	healed and healing linear and loop scars, trunk
FRACTURES	none
INTERNAL INJURIES	subdural hemorrhage
CAUSE OF DEATH	subdural hemorrhage
PRESENTING STORY	"fell from bed"
METHOD OF INJURY	beaten with hand, fists, and belt
REASON FOR INJURY	"wetting and messing pants"

CHAPTER 11
The Community and the Battered Child: A Program for Help

As it stands, grossly abused children are still routinely returned to parents on the promise that the parents will seek help or do better. In a case that received nation-wide attention, a Toronto coroner's jury in July 1977 found month-old Vicky Ellis had died from natural causes, hastened by improper feeding by her parents, Deborah and Brooks Ellis, and possible errors in judgment by social workers. It was the third infant death in the same family. The baby was dead twenty-one days after Judge Norris Weisman decided it was safe to send her home.

On February 9th, Ruth Parry, a social worker at the Family Court Clinic run by the Clarke Institute of Psychiatry, told Judge Weisman she would "stake everything I know" on her conviction that Vicky would be safe in the care of her mother. When the judge announced his decision to take Parry's advice, he commented: "The evidence presented by Ruth Parry was by far the best I've heard in my court" and called it "complete" and "perceptive." But during the inquest, both Coroner Elie Cass and crown attorney Michael Morse suggested that Parry had been "carried away" by the personal challenge of treating the mother, Deborah Ellis, rather than protecting the child. They said she had lost her objectivity.

Parry herself admitted at the inquest that she had done an "inadequate" job of gathering background information on which to base her outspoken support of the decision to let Ellis care for her child.

But Vicky Ellis' life might still have been saved if Judge Weisman had decided to admit one piece of key evidence: a coroner's verdict on Vicky's sister Darlene, which cited "physical and emotional neglect" as a reason for death. Weisman called it "collateral evidence" and ruled it inadmissible.[1]

It is obvious that too often the courts still protect parental rights above those of the child, even when the most flagrant and repeated injustices have been perpetrated. Very often the dispensing of justice rests squarely on the assumption that parents have vast rights over the treatment of children. Rights that go beyond all other relationships involving persons who are not related.

According to Bryon Gero of the Ontario Association of Professional Social Workers, in his report to the Standing Committee on Health, Welfare and Social Affairs, there is

> ample clinical and research evidence to suggest that marital, parent-child and personality difficulties can and do lead to child neglect and ultimately to child abuse. There is also sufficient evidence that environmental factors, such as poverty and inadequate housing can place further stress on less than adequate marriages and personalities. Cumulative stress factors lead to neglect and abuse.
>
> Some parents have never matured enough and some lack sufficient interpersonal resources to equip them for parenting. Others are so engrossed in their own needs that they are simply unable to meet the emotional needs of their children. In these instances children stand a good chance of being rejected, neglected, disturbed or abused through no fault of their own.[2]

Few of us, for instance, would be bold enough to maintain that many children in today's world can function as mothers at the age of thirteen or fourteen, or that the children of such children can be nourished by the social milieu into which they are born, or accommodated by an already overloaded adoption process. In 1975, there were 12,642 births to young women under the age of fifteen in the United States, about the same number as in 1974.[3,4]

For the children who are removed from their parents by social agencies, a whole new series of problems arises. There is a pressing need for good foster-care homes and reliable foster parents, and a need for greater scrutiny of people who are currently acting as foster parents.* An additional point, however, is raised by Kempe, who writes:

> It is regrettable that ever since it was feared some foster homes were becoming a business rather than a vocation, foster parents are offered so little money that many very suitable, but not well-off, foster mothers are working in industry when in fact they should be earning the same kind of money doing what is socially a much more important job. Clearly, we must make good foster care a socially and financially rewarding profession in the years to come.[5]

A plan should be developed for providing a system of foster care service with special training programs for foster parents. It should be based on the needs of the child rather than on the need of the community to shovel children off to anybody who is willing to look after them. It should include special psychiatric or therapeutic treatment for abused children if they are old enough to benefit from it. And more stringent assessment by social agencies should be made to see that foster parents are able to provide the special kind of warmth, love and emotional retraining that these children need.

There is also a need for a considerably closer follow-up of abused children, whether they are placed in foster care homes or have been returned to their parents. These children cannot simply be returned to their homes and forgotten. On-going treatment must continue for both the child and the parents. The parents obviously need therapy and help, and psychiatric or group therapy is often essential in these cases. However, the heavy case loads of psychiatrists and their inability to handle the ever-increasing numbers of people seeking their help makes it very clear that an additional kind of service should be available to these parents.

An innovative program in Denver, Colorado is having good results. Parents are assigned lay people from the community who have volunteered to work with adults who battered their children. These parent aides make themselves available day and night to comfort, console, and give emotional support to the parents. They take on the roles of mothers and fathers to these individuals who never knew or experienced good rela-

---

*A number of children are battered in foster homes.[6-8]

tionships with their own mothers or fathers. These volunteers do not attempt to provide in-depth therapy, but, acting as surrogate parents, do provide emotional warmth and reassurance and an ear for the problems of these individuals. They thereby help to drain off the hostility, loneliness, anger, and rejection that the parents might very well take out on the child. These lay therapists are closely supervised by social workers, psychiatrists and/or pediatricians.[9]

There is no doubt that the whole problem of battered children and battering parents is extremely complex. There are no simple solutions.

It is obvious that the community needs to rescue and treat the abused child and prevent further abuse. Unless each pupil is taught in school all aspects of what it means to be a child, how to feed, care for, and nurture children, it will be impossible to prevent abuse. Further, this information would have to start in pre-school and be carried on throughout the entire schooling in order to be effective. It is long past the time of talking about lessons in parenting; it is time to implement.

The Standing Committee on Health, Welfare and Social Affairs, in response to the question "If the welfare of the child is to be the criterion, what preventive services are needed?", produced the following recommendations:

> First, family planning services are needed and then services for the child from conception onward. Certainly pre-natal services are of the utmost importance.
>
> Among the services suggested by witnesses for the post-natal and pre-school period the Committee was impressed with the concept of the health visitor who visits every child soon after birth as a major preventive tool against child abuse and neglect.
>
> In this connection, the Committee was especially interested in the way in which some of these centres function in other countries, notably in the Scandinavian countries and in Britain. The concept of the "health visitor" has been developed and applied successfully in these centres. We are told this system is also functioning successfully in selected areas in Colorado where Dr. Kempe has been influential in their establishment. The "health visitor" in these centres is a lay person attached to a community clinic, who visits every family where there is a newborn infant. Referrals can be made as necessary to specialists. Such centres are open 24 hours a day, and any parent who wishes it may receive service. In Sweden there is an estimated 80 per cent public voluntary usage of such centres and about 40 per cent in Britain.
>
> The Committee was encouraged to learn that Health and Welfare ministers are interested in the concept of community health centres which offer a wide range of health services and related social services on a 24-hour basis and in whose operation the community participates. A number of these community centres (approximately 74 as of October, 1975) are now operating in Canada. Services offered vary; some centres offer such

services as outreach services, family planning services, pre-natal classes, day-care services and school health programs.

Health services for the infant and young child are of primary importance. Not only are services such as the health visitor a first line of defence, they are also seen as acceptable and welcomed by the public.

Health and Social Service centres are also appropriate agencies to deliver or otherwise provide for respite services for families who need them and for informal or structured programs of education or training in child care. The matter of adult education in child care can and should be shared among a number of community agencies – home-maker services, educational authorities through extension or other courses, family and children's service agencies, provincial and municipal departments of social services, and churches, self-help groups, to mention only a few.

The Committee also emphasizes the need for courses in parenting, child care, home management, and family living in primary, secondary and post-secondary schools. The media could also be much more effective in disseminating practical and high-quality information on these subjects.[10]

AGE	two months
SEX	male
ASSAILANT	mother
RECENT EXTERNAL INJURIES	one small bruise on head
REMOTE EXTERNAL INJURIES	three small healing bruises on head
FRACTURES	skull
INTERNAL INJURIES	congenital hydrocephalus; cerebral contusion
CAUSE OF DEATH	resolving and recent subdural hemorrhage
PRESENTING STORY	"car bed collapsed on him, banging head"
METHOD OF INJURY	struck with fist, banging head against wall
REASON FOR INJURY	"crying at feeding time"

CHAPTER 12
The Police: A Source of Protection for the Battered Child

After looking at the social work approach to child abuse since 1961, I have come to believe that we have failed. Failed to protect the battered child, failed to protect the abused and neglected child, and been much too soft on parents and parents' rights, thus allowing child abuse to continue while we discussed what we should do with abusing parents instead of protecting the abused child. The social work concept has continued to deny that a crime has occurred, therefore denying the victim protection. Child abuse is a crime and must be recognized and treated as such before any real progress can be made in prevention.

The Solicitor General of Canada, in addressing the Standing Committee on Health, Welfare and Social Affairs, said:

> I would like to turn now to one agency which much of the literature on child abuse neglects. Where do the police fit into the scheme of things? I think we should remember at the outset that police officers are always

89

available. They are in the community on a twenty-four hour basis and they are within the reach of anybody with a telephone. I would also point out that the average police officer on patrol duty spends between sixty and eighty per cent of his time as a peace officer providing basic social and other services. Why then should we not use him as part of a multidisciplinary team in both the prevention and handling of cases of child abuse. In some major American cities, the police are very much involved in dealing with child abuse cases and I would suggest that the Committee might like to hear evidence from Sgt. Bob Holmes of the Royal Canadian Mounted Police who has had an opportunity to examine quite closely the work being done by the Los Angeles Police Department in this area.

It must be recognized that there are prejudices operational at the present time between police officers and social workers. Social workers claim that they don't like to get police involved in their cases as the parents accuse them of selling them out to the cops. Police officers make a very similar criticism of social workers except in their case the parents say "you sold my child to the baby snatchers". These accusations may sound crude and they may sound juvenile but they are there and a major obstacle has to be to realize that we are all professionals serving the public and we must help each other. We can no longer say "you are a police officer, this is your job, I am a social worker, this is mine". Too much of the tasking is interchangeable.

A hundred years ago or even fifty years ago, the policeman on the beat maintained a very strong personal relationship with the people in his community. The increased mobility provided by the automobile and modern technology has tended to de-emphasize the preventive aspects of the policeman's role. It is time to recognize that policemen must provide essential support to social services and to give them the kind of training and to deploy them so as to maximize their contribution. There are some impressive experiments in this area now being carried out and I would table for your information a report of a project carried out in the City of London. This particular project is an experiment in family crisis intervention. A number of domestic crisis situations feature some kind of child abuse and I would submit to you that the trained police officer who is investigating a family crisis situation is in a good position both to recognize a case of child abuse and to take appropriate action.

I think there is a very basic need to examine the role of police in the prevention, identification and referral of child abuse cases and to develop the kind of coordination between law enforcement agencies and other social service agencies that will result in maximum utilization of their respective talents and resources. I think the Federal Government may well want to play a role in providing funding to carry out the research and demonstration projects associated with this goal.

One thing we might add is, in police training, in RCMP training, we are now placing a greater emphasis on preventive policing and on such things as family crisis intervention.

As part of our training for family crisis intervention, we are training policemen to better identify cases of child abuse and to work with other professionals. I mentioned in my remarks that we believe there should be a multidisciplinary approach to this, more co-ordination of all the professionals in the field, from the policeman to the social worker to the doctor to the dentist to the daycare worker, and so on."[1]

It has been repeatedly stated in the child abuse literature

that child abusers were abused themselves. Only the law can break this cycle of abuse. The abused child sees that the law does not punish abusing parents. This lesson in social justice does not go unnoticed by abused children who are left to assume that crimes of assault are not punishable in the home, in the school, or in the street. Lawlessness breeds lawlessness and contempt for the law.

Raymond Parnas, Professor at the University of California Law School, writing "The Police Response to the Domestic Disturbance" states:

> The everyday police response to the minor family conflict probably exceeds the total number of murders, aggravated batteries and all other serious crimes....
>
> Although domestic disturbances occur among members of all races, religions and nationalities, police involvement in domestic disturbances tends to take place most often among the poor or uneducated. The "poor, uneducated people appear to use the police in the way that middle-class people use family doctors and clergymen – that is, as the first port of call in time of trouble".[2]
>
> The volume of these minor family conflicts and the high percentage of family members and intimates involved in serious crimes of violence against each other suggest that disturbances might frequently be the prelude to serious crimes of violence.
>
> The report by the President's Commission on Law Enforcement and Administration of Justice states that "family altercations ... are probably the single greatest cause of homicides."[3,4]

Parnas, presenting to the interdisciplinary Second World Conference of The International Society on Family Law in June 1977, stated:

> In the last ten years, stemming from recognition of the peacekeeping role of the police and the exorbitant amount of criminal justice agency time spent on relatively minor family disputes, systematic attempts to deal with this problem have begun....
>
> Violence, no matter how minimal, must remain subject to police intervention. For years a disproportionate number of disturbances, assaults, batteries, uses of deadly or dangerous weapons, mayhems, and homicides have involved family members. Despite the resources necessary and the danger inherent in responding to such calls, no entity other than a police agency has the authority and ability to cope with such volatile situations. Central to the function of the police and the criminal law is the protection of life and limb....
>
> All of the data showing the extent of interfamily violence and the experience of escalation from minimal to aggravated injury indicate that it would be irresponsible governmental action to drop the matter at this point. In fact, however, what we have been doing is to ignore the extremely important preventative, corrective, retributive, incapacitative, and deterrent implications of this early official knowledge of subsequent potential violence. At the very least an adequate record-keeping procedure

must be implemented so that all those responding to subsequent incidents will know of the disputants' prior history so that an appropriate relevant additional response can be made. But even more important than our criminal law's traditional escalation of meaningless slaps on the wrist until too late, is recognition of the need for a breakthrough to the consciousness of the disputants as to the seriousness of their behavior at the outset, not later than the second time around at most....

The law cannot ignore or condone acts or threats of imminent violence. The police are best equipped to protect others and themselves. The law can punish whether by fine, incapacitation, other denials of full liberty, embarrassment, inconvenience, etc. Punishment is a clear statement of the personal responsibility of the offender and the condemnation and retribution by society. It is known that where punishment is to be imposed the criminal process provides the best safeguards that such punishment is imposed on the appropriate person under the most adequate circumstances. Incapacitation prevents repetition during the period of incarceration....

As to the threat of increased violence upon the return of an offender who has been fined, jailed or otherwise sanctioned rather than merely counseled and released as in the past, leniency has not seemed to work to prevent repetition and increased injury up to now....

The criminal law, the police, the prosecutor and the courts should respond to incidents of inter-family violence, not only at the upper levels of violence but at the first minimal signs of trouble. In so doing, the importance of the traditional response of arrest, prosecution and sanction as a sign of public disapproval is emphasized and the protection of all citizens is stressed. In addition, all related existing social services and therapeutic techniques could be retained and new ideas continue to be fostered."[5]

In the past, it has been felt that the trouble with criminal or quasi-criminal provisions would be that they would punish the parent and ignore the victim. This concept rested on the proposition that a criminal court could only punish; it could not change the child's environment. As a result, too often the parent remained unpunished, the child's environment did not change and the abuse continued.

New California legislation, however, recommends re-evaluation of these concepts. Punishment has been re-introduced as an important and necessary legal tool in domestic affairs.[6] While the courts cannot ensure the child an optimum nurturing environment in emotional and/or material terms, the law can protect the child by ensuring that it does not suffer further physical abuse. In the past, it has been the child victim who was removed from their home, not the attacker. Therefore, the child was doubly punished in that it lost its home as well as suffered the assault.

Lack of protective alternatives for abused children in terms of foster placement, group homes, etc., plus the cost to the state in providing for these children, has also been cited as some of the reasons why provinces and states have not wished to enforce criminal actions against parents.

The fact that assaulting parents have not been punished has not been overlooked by the adolescent. Hence, the juvenile offender has often grown up in an environment that has expressed little, if any, respect for the law.

California's new legislation has placed emphasis on punishing abusers and in so doing making it clear that the State of California does not support the assault or abuse of its citizens no matter what their familial relationships.

The California legislation parallels the concept embodied in the Swedish legislation of 1966. Prior to 1966, according to the Swedish *Family Code*, parents were entitled to some extent to use corporal punishment as a means of education. In 1966, however, this section was excluded. Thereby the last parental right to inflict intentional bodily harm on children vanished and the general provision about assault came into force within the field of family law. This implies that only the slightest forms of corporal reprimands fall outside the offence of *assault*. To what extent the legal change also changed the habits in the Swedish population is not yet clear. However, the general enlightened opinion was then and is still that all forms of corporal punishment are contrary to good upbringing of children.[7]

In view of the number of Canadian laws protecting the child, it is easy to believe that every child is fully protected by the state. Overwhelming evidence, however, shows that, in relation to their actual number, very few cases of child abuse are even reported.[8]

Childrens' rights have been completely overshadowed by parental rights and the common law belief that children were not persons but the property of parents. As a result the state, in spite of its vast array of laws, does not implement these laws and is therefore at a complete loss as to how to protect the child. Increasingly, however, the cost both in loss of life and in permanent treatment for those who are victims of violence in the family is causing a reassessment of family rights.

In re-examining the basic principles of due process in child abuse proceedings, including the need for hearing, the need for proper notice, and the right to counsel, it is necessary to recognize that these rules must serve the interests not only of the parents but also of the child.

The results of an abuse proceeding may be a considerable interference by the state in the life of the respondent and their family arrangements. The parents' recognized right to rear children in the manner they deem best may be partially or totally interrupted. Their interest in the abuse proceeding is of sufficient gravity to warrant their representation by counsel.[9] Yet, until recently, legal participation in abuse proceedings was considered by many to be incompatible with the objectives of the family courts.[10] The right of parents to retain counsel was not questioned, but it appears they were not encouraged to do so. Increasing lawyer participation in abuse proceedings should be welcomed by family court judges as beneficial to the family court system. "The right to representation by counsel is not a formality. It is not a grudging gesture to a ritualistic requirement. It is of the essence of justice."[11]

The parent should not be deprived of the custody of the child without due process of law, but neither should the child be deprived of parental nurturing without the same due process. Unless the parent and child are protected from arbitrary exercise of the powers of the state, unrestrained by established principles that recognize and protect the private rights of both the citizen as a child and the citizen as a parent, we are not helping the abused child or protecting the rights of the child or the parents.

The problems regarding the rights of the child and the rights of the parents involve the necessity for both to have proper legal counsel. This may sound too basic to mention. But the fact is that, until recently, in many U.S. jurisdictions, perhaps fewer than 10 per cent of the respondent parents were represented in abuse proceedings.[12] F. M. Fraser notes that in Canada "specific provision is made for legal representation of infant (minor) parents in Ontario. This recognition of a right to counsel should not cease upon the attainment of majority and should be provided for in all jurisdictions. In Nova Scotia the right to counsel is recognized by statute; in practise less than twenty-five per cent of parents have counsel."[13]

Generally we assume that the province, as represented by a child care agency, is acting solely in the best interests of the child, and that the solicitor for the agency represents the child adequately. However, this is not necessarily true where the petitioner is the protective agency, because sometimes the agency's involvement may tend to diminish its ability objectively to weigh the needs of the child against the rights of the parents, or vice versa.[14]

In New York, the court is required to appoint a law guardian whose function is to represent each child who is the subject of protective proceedings. Although in New York these people are called law guardians, they are in fact attorneys and their roles are to act in the interests of the child.[15] The Ontario Family Law Project recommends the adoption of such a procedure in Ontario.[16]

It has been rightly pointed out that giving the child independent legal representation means that the court will be confronted with:

> (a) the child care agency with its lawyer;
> (b) the parents and their lawyer; and
> (c) the child and his or her lawyer.*

To fail to protect the child, however, is to continue to abandon its rights to full protection.

It is for this reason also that Section 43 of the *Criminal Code*† should be removed, thus implying that "only the slightest forms of corporal reprimands fall outside the offence of *assault*."[20] The deletion of Section 43 would place Canadian legislation in line with "The general enlightened opinion ... that all forms of corporal punishment are contrary to the good up-bringing of children."[21]

This opinion was upheld during the interdisciplinary Second World Conference of the International Society on Family Law dealing with Violence in the Family, and was stated in the summary of the Conference proceedings by Judge Victor J. Baum, Trial Judge of the Third Judicial Circuit of Detroit,

---

See the recent and somewhat unfortunate case of Re Helmes.[17]

†*Section 43 states: "Every school teacher, parent or person standing in the place of a parent is justified in using force by way of correction toward a pupil or child, as the case may be, who is under his care, if the force does not exceed what is reasonable under the circumstances."*[18]

Regardless of this authority, Sec. 26 of the Criminal Code *states: "Everyone who is authorized by law to use force is criminally responsible for any excess thereof according to the nature and quality of the act that constitutes the excess."*[19]

Michigan, who was the principal draftsman of the Michigan Child Custody Act. "Certainly one of the highlights of this Conference is a consensus, which is even now gathering momentum, that to eliminate violence within the family, we must first eliminate corporal punishment of children."[22]

Child abuse is cyclical. There are ample data to support the proposition that the abused child grows up to be an abusing parent. In addition, a vast number of juvenile delinquents report severe child abuse in their backgrounds. Studies of adult criminals also report a high incidence of childhood abuse. The cost in social and monetary terms of failing to provide protection for the child clearly indicates the need for a new approach to the questions of family law and the misuse of corporal punishment. It can be argued that unless the law stays the hand of the adult, the child is virtually without protection.

Police officers and the public can no longer ignore the fact that child abuse is a leading cause of infant mortality in Canada and the United States.* The number of reported cases of abuse and neglect has been rising steadily in the last several years. It is uncertain, however, whether the increasing trend reflects an actual increase in the number of children being mistreated or simply an increase in the number of people willing to report. Unfortunately, the incidence of child mistreatment seems to be growing.

*The U.S. National Center on Child Abuse and Neglect lists child abuse as the fifth killer of children in the United States, after accidents, cancer, congenital abnormalities, and pneumonia.[23]

AGE	twenty-one months
SEX	female
ASSAILANT	unknown
RECENT EXTERNAL INJURIES	numerous bruises on face and trunk; laceration of lip; loose teeth
REMOTE EXTERNAL INJURIES	healing contusion, face and bridge of nose
FRACTURES	femur-healed
INTERNAL INJURIES	laceration and contusion, mesentery
CAUSE OF DEATH	laceration of mesentery with hemorrhage
PRESENTING STORY	"fell downstairs"
METHOD OF INJURY	struck by fists in face and abdomen
REASON FOR INJURY	unknown

CHAPTER 13
Saving the Child for the Future

Every adult knows that he or she is not *owned* by his or her parents. But in our culture one must become an adult to realize this. The law still refuses to recognize that parents are only caretakers for the new generation, not owners of the young. If the law is to take effective measures against the battering of children, the law must abandon the assumption that parents have rights of ownership over their infants or children. If the law recognizes the child as an entity, unowned by the parents, the law should cut the child loose from the old Roman *Patria Potestas* (see Chapter 17). Children would then be entitled under law to live in situations which are conducive to optimum health, both mental and physical, just as adults are. This right for the child can be established only by way of legislation and implementation of the law.

Canadian law does not force an adult to remain in an atmosphere dangerous to his or her physical or mental health. What must be remembered, however, is that there was a time when adults were legally bound to remain in situations which were dangerous to both their mental and physical states.

Outright slavery in earlier times, the feudal structures, which tied the serfs to the lands of the nobility, the practice of indenturing servants and, of course, marriage which did not allow divorce and thus legally tied adults to one another are all examples of how the law failed to recognize the rights of the adult. *The law must now recognize the rights of the child independent of the parents' ability to provide these rights.* When this happens the society will have to accept the responsibility of morally and economically providing an optimum existence for all its children. The first duty of the law and society should be to provide full and continuing protection for the child. This does not exclude the concept of therapy as a rehabilitative factor for the parents, which should be developed as fully as possible.

Dr. David G. Gil of Brandeis University directed a study involving an analysis of 1,380 child abuse reports. In his analysis he traced the high level of child abuse in the United States to a widespread acceptance among Americans of the use of physical force as a legitimate procedure in the rearing of children.[1] Because the abuse of children in Canada also rests on this cultural concept of approval for punitive child rearing methods, it may be necessary to challenge this concept by more vigorously enforcing the law.

At some point society must ask why it is battery to strike your neighbour and not battery to strike your child. The concept of not wanting to punish a parent for physical abuse against a child because it may remove him as a breadwinner or because it is "his child" is not consistent with the attitude that the law takes toward that same person if he were to strike his neighbour. In spite of an attitude of deep sympathy for the parents who batter children and a complete awareness of their need for treatment and rehabilitation, the question can still be asked: will the plight of children ever be taken seriously by the public unless the law makes it clear that, regardless of their age, all citizens of Canada fall under the jurisdiction and protection of the law?

Unless the law defends the child against the assaults of parents or caretakers, it is in fact deferring to the old belief in the *Patria Potestas*. The law's course of action should be to punish with fines or imprisonment those parents or caretakers who abuse children. However, the law may still fail the child if it does not provide continuing protection from the attacker who returns after incarceration only to abuse the child again. The law would protect the child better and help the parents more by sentencing abusive parents to periods of therapeutic treatment, plus impressing on them that a recurrence of such behaviour would incur further fines and incarceration.

All citizens have the right to know the law. Therefore, it is necessary to teach the law to everyone. In schools and in the media the laws regarding assaults on children should be explained. Men, women, and children need to know the limits of behaviour that the law in Canada permits toward its citizens.

It is possible for the law to protect the child, treat the parents and, in so doing, change society's traditional attitude toward the rights of parents to use corporal punishment against children as legitimate methods of socialization. This would apply not only in instances of abuse against small children, but would be particularly dramatic in instances of assault against older children. At present the law provides little or no sanctuary for older children who may be consistently assaulted at the hands of their parents. Intervention by the law is extremely rare in these instances, and yet the law should provide full protection for all of its citizens.

Because of the complexity of these questions and the number of social attitudes involving the traditional concepts of family life which give approval to the use of "certain measures" of physical force *as legitimate and appropriate socializing methods within the culture*, it would seem appropriate that a full investigation of all the cultural, legal, economic and emotional aspects of child rights be carried out in order that co-ordinated federal and provincial programs can be developed.

In order to accomplish such an investigation, a Law Commission on the Status of the Canadian Child should be established, and empowered to investigate the entire question of the rights and protection of children.

Canada has the ability and the money to create far more than just adequate institutions to receive children who may have had the misfortune to be born of parents who are emotionally ill or intellectually unequipped to care for them or who really do not want them. Canada has the ability to create institutions which give the very best. This would involve the kinds of artistic, creative and scientific talents which were marshalled to make Expo 67 possible. Major universities produce graduates who are proud to have attended these institutions. It is possible to create child care institutions which would provide the very best in care and instruction, and make possible for the recipients not only the emotional stability and education necessary to live in a complex and changing world, but also the status that attending a good educational institution has traditionally conveyed. People are Canada's most important product and it is to their welfare that society should be putting forth its very best efforts, both intellectually and economically. There *are* answers to the problems of battered children, unwanted children and neglected children.

Schools such as Summerhill have set an example of the kinds of institutions which offer an optimum kind of existence for children who live away from parents. They make it abundantly clear that children are able to cope and thrive in atmospheres which are warm, loving, educationally stimulating and permissive within limits.[2,3] It is not always necessary to place children in nuclear families; the newest studies on kibbutzim make it clear that the children of the kibbutz seem to be hardier physically and stronger emotionally, more well-balanced, more secure and able to behave more appropriately than many of our own middle and upper class children who have received the very best of what our system offers.[4]

Battered and abused children will be the abusive parents of the future unless the Canadian people do something. It may sound unrealistic to say that the battered and abused children of today threaten the society of the future, but this is not as far-fetched as it sounds. In studies of ideologies, personality and attitudes towards war and peace conducted by the Canadian Peace Research Institute, and in almost every article and book in this field, researchers have traced definite patterns.

All these studies taken together would suggest that mental health and social responsibility (including international responsibility) are functions of a relatively permissive and democratic social structure (including childhood discipline), while mental illness and social irresponsibility (including international irresponsibility) are functions of an unduly restrictive and authoritarian social structure (including childhood discipline). Consequently, if we want to change from more compulsive ideologies and personalities to more compassionate ideologies and personalities, we need to change from more repressive disciplines, institutions, procedures, rules and regulations, to those that permit more freedom and encourage more responsibility from early childhood throughout the life cycle.[5, 6-9]

The importance of modelling is a key factor in both the cultural and psychological moulding of children. The effects of brutalization on the lives of individuals are mirrored in the acts of aggression and brutality which take place individually and within the culture at large.*[11-13]

Violence does breed violence. Researchers studied and reviewed family backgrounds over three generations to show that "some abused children become abusive parents of tomorrow. The child who experiences violence as a child has the potential of becoming a violent member of society in the future."[14] The researchers believe that the physician, by reporting child abuse cases to the social agencies for treatment, has "a unique opportunity to interrupt this cycle of violence."[15]

In a pilot study, a consecutive series of one hundred juvenile offenders was interviewed by social workers and psychiatrists. Over eighty per cent of these juvenile offenders gave a history of having been subjected to physical abuse at the hands of their parents during childhood. Approximately forty per cent could recall having been knocked unconscious by one or the other parent.[16,17]

Another study conducted on persons who committed first degree murder illustrates an extreme example of this. In this study, only individuals who had been responsible for a person's death in an impulsive, isolated way were selected. These murderers had no record of any other violent crimes. Six men, imprisoned for life in the Minnesota State Prison, and their parents, were interviewed in an attempt to record what the parents' attitudes and behaviour had been toward the murderer as a child. Two of the men were excluded when it was learned they had been psychotic at the time the murder was committed. The remaining four subjects, however, were found to have suffered almost continual and remorseless brutality at the hands of one parent, while the other parent had remained silent and allowed this to take place.[18]

In his remarks to the Standing Committee on Health, Welfare and Social Affairs, Warren Allmand, former Solicitor General of Canada, stated: "We must worry about the needs and problems of all children and at the same time also be

---

*The literature also suggests that a certain kind of childhood schizophrenia can develop in children who have been exposed to violently abusive parents.[10]

concerned about their rights. I do not believe there is any other group in Canadian society whose rights are as nebulous and as ill-understood as those of children, and I do not think we are very far from the day when we will have to think very seriously about codifying precisely which rights children do or do not have."[19]

The United Nations Declaration of Rights of 1959 states the following: "The child shall enjoy special protection, and shall be given opportunities and facilities, in law and by other means, to enable him to develop mentally, morally, spiritually and socially in a healthy and normal manner and in conditions of freedom and dignity. In the enactment of laws for this purpose, the best interests of the child shall be the paramount consideration."

James A. McGrath (M.P.), in his notes for a brief to the National Task Force Study on the Status of the Child in Canadian Society: The Child as a Citizen, stated on September 17th, 1976:

> It is essential to place firmly in the minds of the public, the idea of children's rights. At the present time, many people are puzzled and bewildered by the concept of children's rights, but it is our task to show that such an idea is not absurd. A child is an individual with certain basic rights and freedoms.
>
> Not long ago, Cuba adopted a *Family Code*. Essentially, this Code acknowledged three things: first, the importance of the family unit; second, the importance of the parent-child relationship, and third, the responsibility of the state to ensure the healthy development of the child. Canada must also take steps that show the value and importance of the family and its role in nurturing future citizens.
>
> In 1885, Canada, following the pattern of Great Britain and the United States, enacted child labour laws to protect children from exploitation. For the first time, children were recognized as citizens. The time has come for us as a nation to recognize in law that children have other rights. In 1959, the United Nations declared by Resolution, the Rights of Children and the responsibility of states to enact laws to ensure a healthy environment which would allow the child to develop physically, mentally, morally, spiritually and socially in a healthy and normal manner and in conditions of freedom and dignity. The Province of British Columbia has before it at the moment a draft Bill of Rights for Children. It is time we had a Canadian Bill of Rights for Children.[20]

In the publication, *The Legal Rights of Children*,[21] it states:

> For several years, countries have provided a variety of services for children in health, welfare, education and justice, but limited were the occasions when experts from these fields, although preoccupied with the welfare of children, have undertaken to promote the rights of children.
>
> Often victims of their parents' deficiencies, tossed about by values tinged by social status, poorly sheltered, handicapped, abandoned, abused

or battered, too many children are left defenseless at a time when their normal development and mental health are compromised.

Faced with this situation, it becomes the duty of a mental health movement to sound the alarm. The Canadian Mental Health Association, the World Federation for Mental Health and the Caribbean Federation have taken this initiative by calling upon experts to study this question publicly, to extend the understanding of children, to promote new legislation and to make available necessary information on the rights of children.

The recommendations in *The Legal Rights of Children* include the following:

1. The rights and welfare of children should be given priority in all national social policy considerations.

2. Whereas malnutrition and inadequate diet contribute to poor mental and physical health, the state should guarantee from conception to seven years of age adequate nutrition as defined by the World Health Organization guidelines.

3. Whereas poverty generally creates marital tension and family breakdown, an adequate guaranteed annual income should be adopted by all governments.

4. Each agency supported by public funds should be required as a precondition for receiving those funds to state its goals in terms that are susceptible to evaluation and to set aside a sufficient portion of its budget to carry out this evaluation.

5. In any appearance before the court where the child's interest may be affected, the child should be represented by one or more competent adults including adequate legal representation, as the exigencies of the case require.

6. The child should have a right to initiate court proceedings in order to obtain emancipation in cases where the parent-child relationship is detrimental.

7. All legislation should be examined to assure that it permits citizens to protect all rights of children. This recommendation is based on a premise that people do want to help and that they do assume responsibility.

8. That we emphasize prevention and continue to develop rehabilitation programs.

9. Citizens should be educated to appreciate all family structures and life styles in society.

10. The laws concerning the administration of justice and welfare should be reviewed by interdisciplinary and interprofessional committees. Sub-committees, assisted by legislative

draftsmen, should be charged with drafting any new laws or amendments to legislation.

11. Judges and other decision makers in the field of juvenile justice and child welfare should receive intensive interdisciplinary training (preferably before their appointment but on a continuing basis). This should include the law, its interpretation and administration; the existing and desirable resources; psychological and social problems; and the processes necessary for arriving at decisions understood and accepted by all parties concerned. There should be funds appropriated for this purpose.

12. Juvenile courts should be required to obtain a pre-trial independent assessment of the family to determine whether or not the jurisdiction of the court should be exercised.

13. We should urge the support of the child advocacy system to promote and safeguard the rights of children.

14. Efforts to instil the public value of mental health among members of the community begin with the organization of school experiences which strongly involve pupils in responsibility for each other, in helping each other, and in working on common projects, preferably of social utility.

15. Compulsory education should be retained for all children regardless of endorsement. It should be defined broadly enough to allow a wide range of experiences inside and outside the school, selected to build competence and awareness on a basis of self-esteem.

16. Industry should reach out to children by providing concrete experiences contributing to their education ("Work experience programs").

17. The schools of a community should be assigned full charge of the educational needs of the community's children, with the authorization to use the most flexible mode of delivery in their services.

18. Children should have the right to reject inappropriate education, and to have access to appropriate alternate experiences.

19. The work of professionals (eg. teachers, social workers, psychiatrists) should be subject to lay scrutiny and regulation as well as collegial control, and promotion on the basis of merit should be stressed to balance the rights of the child against those of the professional.

20. Educators whose intimate work with children has the

essential function of fostering their self-development rather than bringing to bear specialized skills (eg. those of special educators for exceptional children in treatment centres, residences, group homes, and foster homes) should be afforded recognition.

21. Police services should be integrated along with educational, health, and social services in their communities with a view to early prevention of harm to the child's development.

22. Professionals in charge of implementing the rights of children should be trained systematically in the social manipulation of power in a democracy.

23. No agency, public or private, should be licensed to place or receive children unless it is also equipped and authorized to offer preventive services (eg. day care, preventive counselling, or homemaker services).*

*The recommendations have been listed in the order that they were submitted. They express the wish of each participant who formulated them. Even though the participants did not have an executive mandate to implement these recommendations, it was believed that they should be published in order to invite existing services to take note of them and to take action whenever possible. The Canadian Mental Health Association continues its action for the legal rights of children through its programs and/or in collaboration with other organizations.

TYPICAL CASE PROFILE

AGE	eighteen months
SEX	male
ASSAILANT	mother
RECENT EXTERNAL INJURIES	numerous bruises and abrasions, head and trunk; laceration of lip
REMOTE EXTERNAL INJURIES	healed pattern burn on buttocks; healed linear scars, trunk and extremities
FRACTURES	none
INTERNAL INJURIES	contusion, brain; subdural hemorrhage
CAUSE OF DEATH	subdural hemorrhage
PRESENTING STORY	"fell from potty chair"
METHOD OF INJURY	placed on gas burner; beat with stick and hands
REASON FOR INJURY	"wet pants"

CHAPTER 14
The Broad Spectrum of Cultural Violence

Violence waits in the dusty sunlight of a tenement yard and in the shadows of a distraught mind. Violence draws nearer in the shouts of a protest march and in ghetto rumblings. Violence erupts from Mace-sprinkled billy clubs and a homemade Molotov cocktail. Violence of war explodes the peace it promises to bring. Hourly reports of violence bring numbness, shock, confusion, sorrow. We live in a violent world.[1]

A culture which ignores its own institutionalized violence may ultimately trigger its own destruction. Canadian society ignores the brutalization and violence which is routinely inflicted on children by parents, but it also ignores the brutalization and violence that is portrayed by television exploiters, by sexual-sadistic pulp magazines, and by cheap journalism in newspapers. By permitting television, magazines, newspapers, and funnies to exploit and extol the virtues of violence, society feeds violence. As far back as 1967, a report of the Federal Communications Commission of the United States estimated that between the ages of five and fourteen the average American child

106

witnesses the violent destruction of thirteen thousand human beings on television. Since that time reports indicate that violence on television has increased. One can only speculate as to the number of human beings destroyed before the eyes of the public at present.[2]

In 1969, The Voice of Women, monitoring the two Canadian television networks for a thirty-hour period, tabulated a total of twenty murders, sixty-eight killings, fifty-nine injuries, fifty-five fights, ten bombings, and thirty-seven conflicts between criminals and lawmen. This amounts to a total of two hundred and forty-nine violent conflicts in a thirty-hour period, or a violent conflict occurring approximately once every seven minutes.[3] More recently, the Ontario Royal Commission on Violence in the Communications Industry and its American counterpart have ample documentation of the effects of television violence.

To deny the reality of modelling is to deny the impact of culture. People would not speak English if they did not hear others speak it. People would not eat with a particular set of manners if they did not model themselves after the way they see others eat around them. They would not dress in a particular style if they did not model themselves after those who set the styles. Life is a series of modellings after those who are either chosen as heroes or unconsciously emulated. In this regard, adults and children alike are affected by the kinds of behaviour they witness.[4]

This phenomenon is illustrated by a study of nursery school children conducted at Stanford University and reported by Dr. Albert Bandura. Three groups of children were exposed to three different sets of experiences. One group saw a cartoon filled with violence; another saw a movie about flowers; the third witnessed an actual fight staged in their classroom. Immediately after reviewing these stimuli each group was placed in a room with the usual nursery toys plus a large punching doll. The behaviour of the children was observed. The group which had viewed the flower movie played with a random group of toys, with the more aggressive children hitting the doll. The group which had seen the real fight exhibited more aggressive behaviour, with a few more children knocking over the doll. In the group which had watched the cartoon, almost all of the children hit the doll with a more intense degree of aggression and hostility.[5,6]

The defenders of brutality on television point out that the good guy always wins in the end. But studies indicate that the dominant message that comes through to the child and the adult viewer is not that right always wins, but on the contrary that violence is the only method that works.[7] In addition, those who lose may be seen as bad and weak *because they are losers*, just as readily as they are seen to lose because they are bad or weaker. It is really beside the point whether or not the hero wins in the end; the fact is that violence is the dominant theme which we show to both the small and large viewers.

Dr. Richard A. Walters of the University of Toronto asked adult and adolescent males to help with a study that was presumably concerned with the effects of punishment on learning. The adult participants were provided with an electric shock apparatus through which they could administer shocks at varying lengths and degrees of intensity to adolescent learners whenever they made mistakes. Before starting the experiment the adult participants themselves sampled a few shocks to become familiar with the pain levels corresponding to the different shock intensities. Unknown to the adult participants, the adolescent learners were instructed to make periodic and intentional errors on the tests. Also, unknown to the participants, the electrodes had been disconnected so that the learners were, in fact, receiving no shocks at all. That is, the people who were giving the shocks were not aware that the boys who were pretending to learn were actually faking pain they should have felt corresponding to the shock that they received. In the second part of the study, half the participants were shown the switchblade knife scene from the movie *Rebel Without a Cause*, while the other half saw a short film about picture making. Immediately afterwards they all repeated the shock administration test and the resulting change in the participants' willingness to administer pain-producing shocks was noted. The people who had watched the picture-making film gave the learner weaker shocks, but the people who had seen the very violent switchblade scene from the movie, gave longer and more powerful shocks, and had the electrodes been connected they would have caused the learners considerable pain. Moreover, these participants showed a pronounced increase in aggression and hostility on an objective personality test which they were given.[8]

The theory that exposure to aggression drains off innate

aggression into harmless avenues which relieve the society of the otherwise pent-up or built-up aggression within an individual, is strongly refuted by many scientists. Experiment after experiment shows quite the contrary, that the more exposure there is to violence the more violence, either direct or indirect, there will be.[9]

Dr. John P. Spiegel, Director of the Lemberg Center for the Study of Violence at Brandeis University and adviser to the American National Committee on the Causes and Prevention of Violence, says,

> Violence is not a basic instinct like sex or hunger. It isn't a pressure that comes from within and then has to be released .... Violence is a cultural style. What we must do is to reverse the style.[10]

When asked if the new sexual freedom was the cause for violence, his reply was:

> Not really, even though people often get confused about this, we have always been an open society in which the right to change our rules, sexual or otherwise, and to develop new patterns of democratic living has been a privilege. This is the meaning of our country.[11]

Asked if affluence was responsible for today's violence, he replied: "Only in so far as it affects inequality of opportunity."[12]

Asked whether today's trouble can be blamed on permissiveness in the home or on progressive education, he replied:

> I don't think so. One of our permissiveness problems is inconsistency in parents. Many overly strict mothers and fathers think that all they have to do is lay down the law to their children as if this in itself would induce respect. But what a child respects is not the words, but the behaviour of parents. The old-fashioned, heavy authoritarian approach is generally no answer. Actually over-strictness often works the other way. Sometimes it produces a compliant and frightened child, sometimes a rebellious child. But it doesn't produce a child who knows how to live in a world that is constantly changing. You have to train your children to live in a world that will be different from the one in which you grew up. Naturally extreme permissiveness is as bad as extreme authoritarianism. A golden mean, a middle ground, is the wisest in raising a healthy, well-adjusted child. Children do not need many rules, but they do need to know what the rules are and that those rules will be enforced consistently, not punitively.[13]

When asked what effect the emphasis on violence in movies, television and other entertainment has on children, he said:

> Experiments by psychologists tend to support what I suspect. That we live in an atmosphere in which children are overexposed to violent, visual stimuli. One unfortunate effect is that this is a kind of implicit instruction to a child. If you get too frustrated, get violent. Another is the tendency to

raise a child's expectation to *look* for violent stimuli. It is like habituation to anything. If you are exposed to it for a long time, you come to expect it and in fact want it.[14]

To pretend that violence is part of our biological make-up is to become an apologist for violence.[15-17] To deny cause and effect is to be naive. The only rational approach to the question of battered children and battering parents, is to accept the cause and effect of both the battering and the deprivation of love on both the parents and the child.

In a recent poll taken by the *National Enquirer*, people were asked what should be done with parents who battered, abused, tortured and maimed their children. Here are some of the answers:

"The parents should be killed or tortured. Anyone who ill-treats children in a vicious way should get the same treatment themselves."

"I'd toss child beaters into solitary confinement for six months and just give them bread and water. There's no sense in coddling a person who commits bodily harm on a child."

"I think the parents should be treated as murderers."

"Those adults who would put a lighted cigarette to a child should be burned themselves and locked up for a long time."

"Any adult who would lower himself to beat an innocent child should be subject to the most severe punishment that's possible under law. The child also should be taken away forever."

"Punishment should be made to fit the crime. I wouldn't say mutilate or torture people, but they certainly should go to jail for many years. It's the only way to deal with them."

"I think sentences should be stronger. I don't think the children should be given back to parents who abuse them."

"Anyone who would injure a defenseless child should be punished in kind. If a parent breaks a kid's arm, then the parent should have his arm broken. Swift punishment is the answer."

"I absolutely despise child beaters. That's the most unforgivable crime. I recommend very severe punishment for all child beaters, men or women. I suggest that they be jailed permanently and that their children be taken away from them for good."[18]

Society still functions on the old, authoritarian concept of an eye for an eye, a tooth for a tooth, and fails to see that this will help neither the child nor the parent. The fact that many adults have so little insight and so little understanding about parents who batter their children discloses the primitiveness of our culture.

> The need is not really for more brains, the need is now for a gentler, a more tolerant people than those who won for us against the ice, the tiger and the bear.[19]

AGE	two years
SEX	female
ASSAILANT	father
RECENT EXTERNAL INJURIES	numerous bruises, face and abdomen; post-mortem burns, lower trunk and legs
REMOTE EXTERNAL INJURIES	healed circumscribed scars, head and lower lip
FRACTURES	none
INTERNAL INJURIES	contusions, brain and lung; laceration, liver
CAUSE OF DEATH	laceration of liver with hemorrhage
PRESENTING STORY	"found in bath tub"
METHOD OF INJURY	struck by fists; banged head on tub
REASON FOR INJURY	"splashed water"

CHAPTER 15
Soft-Core Abuse: A Cultural Way of Life

Reference has been made earlier (Chapter Three) to the acceptance by many parents of physical violence as a legitimate method of child training. Drs. B. F. Steele and C. B. Pollock enlarge upon this as follows:

> There seems to be an unbroken spectrum of parental action toward children ranging from the breaking of bones and fracturing of skulls through severe bruising to severe spanking and on to mild "reminder pats" on the bottom. To be aware of this, one has only to look at the families of one's friends and neighbours, to look and listen to the parent-child interactions at the playground and the supermarket, or even to recall how one raised one's own children or how one was raised oneself. The amount of yelling, scolding, slapping, punching, hitting and yanking acted out by parents on very small children is almost shocking. Hence, we have felt that in dealing with the abused child we are not observing an isolated, unique phenomenon, but only the extreme form of what we would call a pattern or style of child rearing quite prevalent in our culture.[1]

In a discussion of battered children it becomes necessary to differentiate between the out-and-out child batterer and the parents who, *as a matter of course, carry out a fairly consistent amount of abuse upon their children*. This abuse is carried out in a routine way and is simply unquestioned. It is regarded as the most efficient manner of getting obedience. To describe this form of child abuse I use the term *soft-core abusers* to differentiate them from the hard-core batterers.

Much of our modern knowledge about child rearing has been researched and documented to a point where there is little doubt of its reliability or validity.[2-9] Yet in spite of the vast amount of research done in the area of child development, North American parents are still confused about what they can expect from children, and strongly believe in the necessity of using force to maintain discipline. This confusion arises from the fact that the body of knowledge about child rearing must compete with an intracultural way of life which supports violence and punishment as right and proper within the culture as a whole.

An interesting example occurred during a child abuse trial in Colorado involving a man who had severely beaten and injured his children with a stick and a wooden spoon. Ten of the first twelve people drawn out of the hat for jury duty were challenged and dismissed by the district attorney because they said they too used sticks and belts to discipline their children.[10]

The problem of soft-core abuse, then, is based on the belief held in North America, among other places, that striking children is acceptable and the concept that force and corporal punishment are important adjuncts for maintaining our society and the North American way of life. This attitude is based on tradition and ignorance. It is this larger cultural concept which must be attacked before any real changes in the overall treatment of children can be realized. This, of course, involves a complete examination, not only of child rearing practices, but of cultural practices in general which support and reinforce punitive child-rearing methods.

Dr. David Gil, in the conclusion of his book, *Violence against Children*, states:

> Education tends to recreate a society in its existing image, or to maintain its relative status quo, but it rarely if ever creates new social structures. Violence against children in rearing them may thus be a functional aspect of socialization into a highly competitive and often violent society, one that puts a premium on the uninhibited pursuit of self-interest and that does not put into practice the philosophy of human cooperativeness which it preaches on ceremonial occasions and which is upheld in its ideological

expressions and symbols. The elimination of violence from American child-rearing philosophy and practice seems therefore to depend on changes in social philosophy and social reality toward less competition and more human cooperativeness, mutual caring, and responsibility.[11]

As a first step, the Canadian government should develop comprehensive legal sanctions against the use of corporal punishment in rearing children. The federal and provincial governments should outlaw the use of corporal punishment in schools, juvenile courts, correctional institutions and other child-care facilities.* Specifically, section 43 of the Criminal Code, which currently permits physical punishment of children, should be amended.[12]

Children should receive the same protection against physical attack as the law provides for adults. Moreover, these amendments are likely to affect, to a degree, child-rearing attitudes and practices in Canada. They would symbolize society's rejection of violence against children. The present disinclination to adopt child-rearing methods that do not include corporal punishment rests on the unfounded idea that there are no alternatives to punishment. Dr. David Gil addresses himself to this in *Violence against Children*. He states:

> To avoid misinterpretation, it should be noted here that rejecting corporal punishment does not imply favoring unlimited permissiveness in rearing children. To grow up successfully, children require a sense of security that is inherent in nonarbitrary structures and limits. Understanding adults can establish such structures and limits through love, patience, firmness, consistency and rational authority. Corporal punishment seems devoid of constructive educational value, since it cannot provide the sense of security and non-arbitrary authority. Rarely, if ever, is corporal punishment administered for the benefit of the attacked child, for usually it serves the immediate needs of the attacking adult who is seeking relief from his uncontrollable anger and stress. And finally, physical attack by an adult on a weak child is not a sign of strength, for it reflects lack of real authority, and surrender to the attacker's own uncontrollable impulses.[13]

Because the problem of soft-core abuse is based on tradition and ignorance, it can be dealt with in a manner consistent with our current methods of public education. Specific and direct attacks on the question of child abuse could also be carried out in the form of commercials as well as in more general informational approaches to the problems of child rearing. For instance, spot commercials could be made clearly stating that if a

---

Metropolitan Toronto has recently abolished the use of corporal punishment in its schools.

114

person even casually strikes a small child on the head, the result might be very serious ear, eye, or brain damage.[14] Other spot announcements could make it quite clear that, even in play, a child picked up by the arms or by the legs and bounced around may suffer loosening of the arm or leg sockets and very possibly permanent damage to the joints. "Deformities such as bowlegs, knock knees and other bone changes resulting in arthritic changes are now more frequently recognized than previously as the result of inflicted injuries suffered earlier by the child."[15] People must know that children are not nearly as tough and robust as was once thought, but on the contrary are quite fragile. Public service commercials could make it clear that being struck on the head or yanked on the arm may cause permanent damage. This type of information can be taught very effectively through simple programming. Television could present an abundance of exciting programs about childhood and the physiology of the child which explained all about toilet training, eating habits, sex, and all there is to know about being parents.

It is possible, in fact, to instruct parents in the vital information which they so desperately need. Also needed is a primer on child rearing that presents what one can and cannot do in the rearing of children as clearly and definitely as the ABC's. This can be taught in newspapers and magazines as well as over the television and radio. It is necessary however to go one step further than that. This information should be taught through primary school into high schools, and, as well, in the universities.

A curriculum could be set up which would include textbooks, lectures, movies, and teaching auxiliaries, to deal with the whole question of punishment as a child-rearing method. The material would cover what it means to be a human being, how to care properly for human beings, and also how to treat human beings from birth to the time they enter school and, most importantly, how to nurture human beings so that they may nurture others. It is not good enough that our universities only have departments of home economics; we must have departments of human development.[16] These courses should not be just for women, but for men and women. These steps would make it clear to all people, young and old, that it is incorrect to raise children in anything other than a way which promotes health and happiness, and which supports the individual and the individual's ability to lead the good life.*

As it now stands, the pediatrician is too often aware only of the physical and nutritional health of the child. The pediatrician himself, as an individual, is not necessarily aware of what comprises a good or bad method of child rearing from a psychological or environmental point of view. But such gaps of knowledge should no longer be tolerated. As individuals, people are dependent upon experts with specialized fields, but people are not pieces and hunks. A person is not just a liver, a heart or a brain. People are total organisms. Therefore they need experts who are aware of whole structures and who take into account the effect that each specialization has upon the other. Society must now demand that the experts become generalists as well as specialists, or else that specialists come together and pool their information in order to satisfy our desperate need for integrated knowledge.[17] This should not be difficult to accomplish in the area of child rearing.

*For excellent recommendations for a comprehensive program dealing with child abuse, see D. G. Gil, Violence Against Children, Cambridge: Harvard University Press, 1970, Chapter 6.

AGE	eight months
SEX	female
ASSAILANT	mother
RECENT EXTERNAL INJURIES	numerous bruises and abrasions, head and trunk
REMOTE EXTERNAL INJURIES	numerous healing bruises over trunk and extremities
FRACTURES	skull — recent; ribs — recent
INTERNAL INJURIES	contusion, brain; subdural, epidural hemorrhage
CAUSE OF DEATH	intracranial hemorrhage
PRESENTING STORY	"fell out of crib"
METHOD OF INJURY	struck by hand, fist and shoe
REASON FOR INJURY	"cried too much"

CHAPTER 16
The Rights and Limits of Parenthood

North Americans experience a great deal of confusion about the meaning of authority and the roles and functions of people in authority.[1] The children born into this culture are subjected to all the vicissitudes of society's inability to deal with the problems of authority, whether at home, at school or within the society at large.[2]

Just as freedom requires limits, so does the exercise of authority. We want to give children freedom, but not a licence to destroy themselves or others. We want to give parents authority, but not licence to commit murder, to brutalize, to embarrass, to tease, to corrupt or to abuse in any form. Unfortunately our method of raising children not only permits but encourages some of these things.[3,4] Parents are not necessarily good parents simply because they are parents.[5] Paternity and maternity are biological functions only. People can be trained to be extremely good parents. People can be trained to be extremely bad parents. This is a fact that studies in anthropology and psychology have established. This information imposes upon us the necessity to examine quickly what it is that we are doing, not only as a culture but as individuals. It would be true to generalize and say that our culture maintains a bad method of child rearing.

Other cultures, such as the Aleuts, the Arapesh, the Lepchas, the Pygmies, the Eskimos, and some North American Indian tribes, do not abuse their children.[6,7]* These societies "do not dominate over, hurt or kill one another or their neighbours, though they possess the weapons to do so."[8] Authority is not in itself a bad thing. It is a necessary part of human and social relationships. North American society believes that it cannot have obedient children unless parents are prepared to use physical punishment. Having once linked obedience to physical punishment, our society invests in its authorities the right to punish in order to obtain obedience.

When examining the question of the child in the home, there should be no confusion as to who has authority: the parent has. The question is whether or not the parent is fit to have authority. Does he have the information qualifying him to exercise authority? Is he emotionally stable so that he can carry out the role of being the authority? Is the parent in fact able to understand what his authority permits him and what it does not?

Society must make it clear that being a parent does not give one licence to punish in ways which are hateful, cruel and sick. Being a parent does not give one the right to seek release from emotional suffering by way of perpetrating atrocities on one's children.

Brutalization of children is far more normal in the North American culture than people have previously dared to admit. Attitudes which support this method of child rearing are maintained at almost every level of interaction in the society.

A prime example is the commonly held belief that anything that threatens authority is bad. This belief holds that all authority is good because it *is* the authority, or to put it more correctly, because it wears the badge of authority. As a result,

*See William N. Stephens, The Family in Cross-cultural Perspective, *New York: Holt, Rinehart and Winston, 1963, pp. 370-376.*

the society spends a great deal of time, effort and research in maintaining systems of authority, often without examining whether those systems are in themselves necessary or correct.[9]

Deference to authority in North America is taught in the home, in the school, in the church, and in almost every social organization.[10] North American culture does not train its children or its adults to be thinking or creative individuals, but rather to obey. The dominant message within the home, school and social organization is adherence to rules and compliance with authority. More and more terrifying examples of this are emerging from the studies carried out by various researchers in many different disciplines.

One of the most revealing was that carried out at Yale University by Stanley Milgram.[11] The point of the study was to see how far participants were prepared to obey the instructions set by an authority figure. The participants were led to believe that the scientists conducting the experiment were important people who should be obeyed. The following excerpt from a chapter entitled "Dissent and Rebellion in the Laboratory," in Charles Hampden-Turner's *Radical Man*, describes what occurred.

Milgram set up an experimental procedure which ostensibly studied the effect of punishment on memory and learning. In reality degrees of obedience to the command to torture a third party were being measured. Pairs of "volunteers" – which in fact included one genuine volunteer and one confederate of the experimenter – were divided into "trainers" and "learners." In each case the genuine volunteer was the "trainer" and the confederate was the "learner." Both received $4.50 in payment before the experiment began. The "trainer" was then shown an electrical switching apparatus replete with blue and red lights and thirty levers marked 15 volts, 30 volts, 45 volts, etc. up to and including 450 volts. He was invited to test the apparatus by giving himself a small 45 volt shock (which in fact came from a low voltage battery).

The "purpose" of the experiment was explained to him as follows. The "learner" will be given a series of paired words: later when only one word of an original pair is repeated he must remember the other word. If he remembers correctly no shock is given. If he makes a mistake, a series of *escalating* shocks is administered following each mistake. This will enable the experimenter to discover how much pain is associated with the greatest learning. Then comes the following general procedure.

The "trainer" watches the "learner" being strapped into an electric chair. While doing this the experimenter observes that the shocks can be "extremely painful but leave no permanent tissue damage." Electrode paste is smeared on the subject's hand "to avoid blisters and burns." The "trainer" takes up his position behind the switching apparatus where he can hear but not see the "learner," and the experiment begins. According to a prearranged schedule the "learner" makes repeated mistakes which require the trainer to shout "30 volts!" "45 volts!" etc. and then pull down the lever with that marking upon it. The "learner" pretends to feel the shock in the following gradations.

At 75 volts he gives a light grunt. At 120 volts he shouts out that the shocks are becoming painful. At 135 volts he groans painfully. At 150 he demands to be released "Get me out of here. I refuse to go on!" At 180 he shouts that he cannot stand the pain and repeatedly asks to be released until at 270 volts he screams in agony. At 300 he screams that he will not continue the test. The "trainer" is then told that failure to answer is equivalent to a mistake and that higher shocks must be administered. At 315 volts the "learner" repeats his refusal and in fact ceases to perform in the test. He then shrieks and struggles with increasing intensity with every shock up to 450 volts. The experiment is designed to measure at what stage the "trainer" will rebel.

The levers are elaborately marked not only with the voltage but with legends like, "strong shock," "very strong," "intense shock," "extremely intense," "Danger! severe shock," and "XXX." Later it was found that virtually all "trainers" believed the situation. Although a panel of psychiatrists predicted that only 4% would go beyond 300 volts, in fact 78% did so, and although the psychiatrists predicted that only 1/10th of 1% would go to 450 volts, 65% did so. Originally the experiment was set up with no voice audible but only desperate knocking sounds on the wooden cubicle in which the "learner" sat. In this condition so many shocked their victim to the bitter end that cries of increasing agony had to be added, as well as increasing degrees of proximity between "learner" and "trainer," in order to produce a large enough sample of dissenters. Nearly 30% would continue to torture their victim to the end while grappling with him and *holding his squirming hand down upon the shock plate*, while he screamed about a weak heart!

However, very few subjects enjoyed inflicting the pain. Nearly all were highly agitated and pleaded with the experimenter to let them stop. He repeated monotonously "the experiment requires that you continue," and where this and harsher commands were not enough to achieve compliance, his final words were: "You have no choice, you *must* go on."

The degree of obedience seemed incredible to Milgram and his associates, and incredible to the psychiatrists and the scientific fraternity. All this was before Vietnam.[12]

This study on obedience demonstrates the degree to which people have been trained to *respond unthinkingly to a command from a person who is in a position of authority*. Concomitantly, failure to respond to a command of authority appears to these people as a serious breach of discipline.

In one aspect of the pathology of child battering a similar process takes place. The people in the laboratory responded to the demand from an external authority to punish a learner who was unable to perform correctly. In the case of a child batterer the demand to punish for failure to obey comes from an internalized authority which was instilled in the parent during his or her own child rearing. The parent punishes the infant or child for failure to obey. If the punishment does not bring forth the desired response, the parent is commanded by his internalized authority to escalate the punishment.*

In the experiment the demands of the scientist-authority were not questioned, just as the battering parent and the complying parent do not question their demands upon the child. What goal could be so important as to require the torture of individuals for failure to achieve that goal or to obey a command? It is, however, normal in North American society to place more value on the achievement of goals and compliance with the demands of authority than upon the well-being of individuals.

While the general public is prepared to say that child battering is terrible, in the next breath most people still hesitate to condemn spanking or striking children when these actions are linked to the authority of parents in the home. The belief that we should do nothing to diminish the authority of parents lends support to those parents who perpetrate acts of brutality upon children. In view of the fact that parents are among the major killers and maimers of North American children, it becomes imperative to recognize that we must not continue to allow parents to have this almost unlimited authority over children.

It is the unconditional authority of parents which must be challenged. Facing this reality, however, threatens our present structure, and I suspect that an underlying fear of challenging the traditional authority of the parents has caused responsible members of society to shy away from the whole question of the battered and abused child. Doctors, lawyers, neighbours, teachers, politicians, and even social welfare agencies are, as yet, not prepared to demand comprehensive child-care legislation which would, of necessity, challenge the authority of the parent in our society.

The recent awareness of the degree of violence perpetrated against children does not indicate that this is a new phenomenon in our society. We seem to have an inexhaustible capacity for surprise when longstanding abuses are brought to our immediate attention.

Charles Hampden-Turner, in his excellent book *Radical Man*, states the case most eloquently and clearly:

In Dr. Gil's study nearly 63% of his cases involved incidents developing out of disciplinary action taken by caretakers who responded in uncontrollable anger to real or perceived misconduct of the child. [13]

Our culture is always "discovering" things which have been there for centuries without stirring our anger and compassion. The starving children in Mississippi and Appalachia have been there for hundreds of years but only recently have we chosen to see them. Earlier generations tolerated with equanimity the flogging of mental patients and the lynching of black Americans. Charles Grenville, the English diarist observed some small boys being hanged at Tyburn and "was astonished by the incomprehensible attitude of some of the boys sentenced to be hanged. Never did I see boys cry so!" As the Second World War broke over Europe Arthur Koestler wrote of the fascist horror he had seen, suffered and warned against for years. "Perhaps it is we, the screamers, who react in a sound and healthy way to the reality which surrounds us, whereas you are the neurotics who totter around in a screened fantasy world because you lack the capacity to face the facts. Were it not so, this war would have been avoided, and those murdered within sight of your day-dreaming eyes would still be alive."[14]

AGE	eighteen months
SEX	male
ASSAILANT	sibling (age fifteen)
RECENT EXTERNAL INJURIES	numerous bruises on abdomen
REMOTE EXTERNAL INJURIES	numerous linear scars on extremities
FRACTURES	none
INTERNAL INJURIES	lacerations, liver and mesentery
CAUSE OF DEATH	laceration of liver with hemorrhage
PRESENTING STORY	"found dead in crib"
METHOD OF INJURY	beaten with fists
REASON FOR INJURY	"would not eat his food"

CHAPTER 17
A History of Abuse

Infanticide, child abandonment and child sacrifice, as well as neglect and the brutal treatment of children, have been a part of the history of many cultures. Sometimes child abuse is a socially conditioned response. It is plain that the hideous custom of binding the feet of young women in China, which was widely practised until the Communist take-over in 1948, was cruel and crippling but nevertheless socially sanctioned and was carried out by parents with the best of intentions towards their children.

Infanticide too has been a very common and very old practice which was based on the needs and limitations of the community.[1,2]

Mutilation of children may also be based on culturally conditioned attitudes about religion, beauty or cleanliness. Children have always been the victims of mutilation practices. The most common site for mutilation has been the sex organs.[3] For example, circumcision is still performed by civilized people in spite of its questionable value.[4] It is probably the oldest surgical procedure on record, having been practised as a religious rite since the Stone Age.*[5] Parents have also mutilated children for economic reasons. The practice among beggars of mutilating their children in grotesque ways was common throughout Europe and Asia.

Socially sanctioned whipping and beating of children has a history which goes back beyond the record of historians. However it is known that five thousand years ago in Sumer there was an official whip bearer who held a prominent position in the Sumerian educational system.[6] Brutal physical punishment has been a practice of teachers and parents which in turn found justification in religious beliefs and moral attitudes, as well as in legal codifications. The philosophy of "spare the rod and spoil the child" was expressed in the Old Testament and reiterated in 1633 in the *Bibliotheca Scholastica*.[7] Beatings to drive out the devil were a form of psychiatric treatment especially applied to children, particularly where epilepsy was attributed to demonical possession.[8] Many of the Protestant reformers of the seventeenth century viewed children as basically evil. Calvin dictated that only by complete breaking of the will could the young child be "saved" from his inborn evil spirit.[9]

This emphasis on punishment has prevailed throughout the schools of Europe and also formed the basis for school systems in North America.[10,11] As a result, educational reformers from Roger Ascham and Loyola in the sixteenth century, through Locke in the seventeenth century,[12] to Bertrand Russell,[13] John Dewey,[14] and A. S. Neill[15] in the twentieth century, to mention only a very few, have pleaded for more enlightened and less punitive attitudes in the educational system.

Rousseau said, "Let us speak less of the duties of children and more of their rights."** But historically, heavy demands

*In 1975 the American Academy of Pediatrics wrote: "Circumcision of the newborn male cannot be considered an essential component of adequate total health care" (see note 5). The Academy ordered a study after controversy developed over a 1971 report by another committee which said, without elaboration, that it did not think there was medical justification for routine circumcision.

The Academy noted that circumcision prevents cancer of the penis, also that this form of cancer is relatively uncommon. They stressed evidence that good hygiene provides as much, or nearly as much, protection.

**It is interesting to note, however, that Rousseau abandoned his own children.

124

have been made on very young children.[16] Often children were bred for the sole purpose of working for the benefit of their parents. The long history of slavery has included the enslavement of children as a flourishing practice in many countries. Infant girls were sold to be raised as prostitutes, and boys to work.[17] All of this has been possible because many cultures believe that children are the property of parents, to be done with as the parents choose. In other words, the concept of slavery has traditionally applied to children.

The *Patria Potestas* endowed the Roman father with the privilege to sell, abandon, devour, kill, offer in sacrifice, or otherwise dispose of his offspring. Even in adulthood, when the children were in the father's house, they could be sold into bondage, tortured or killed. "In the Forum, the Senate or the camp, the adult son of a Roman citizen enjoyed the public and private rights of a person; in his father's house he was a mere thing, confounded by the laws with the movables, the cattle and the slaves, whom the capricious master might alienate or destroy without being responsible to any earthly tribunal."[18]*

In Henry VIII's time, child labour was instituted as a method of eliminating poverty, and children as young as five were apprenticed without parental consent.[20] The workhouse in the last decade of the seventeenth century caused the death of many children through overwork and terrible conditions. The industrial revolution in the latter half of the eighteenth century transformed child labour into outright slavery. Children from five years of age upwards worked sixteen hours a day, often with irons riveted around their ankles to keep them from running away. They were beaten and starved and many died as a result of occupational diseases. Some committed suicide. Very few survived for any length of time.[21,22]

In England the first factory act was passed by Parliament in 1802, and although it prohibited the pauper apprentice system,

*Bertrand Russell in The History of Western Philosophy *outlines the philosophical foundation of this parental "right": "Aristotle's opinions on moral questions are always such as were conventional in his day. On some points they differ from those of our time, chiefly where some form of aristocracy comes in. We think that human beings, at least in ethical theory, all have equal rights, and that justice involves equality; Aristotle thinks that justice involves, not equality, but right proportion, which is only 'sometimes' equality.*

The justice of a master or a father is a different thing from that of a citizen, for a son or slave is property, and there can be no injustice to one's own property."[19]

it did not challenge the traditional rights of parents over their children. Thus children under the supervision of their parents could still be sent to the mills to work twelve hours a day. In the mills they were often brutally whipped with leather thongs by supervisors. Occasionally children were plunged head-first into cisterns of cold water to keep them from falling asleep at their machines.[23]

In seventeenth- and eighteenth-century England children were subject to the same penalties as adults for crimes, some being punished by death sentences or banishments to prison colonies. The early colonists regarded incorrigibility as just cause for the death penalty for children.

The vestiges of these old traditions can still be seen in Canadian, British and American law. The very old traditional *Patria Potestas* idea of ownership, for instance, is still very much reflected in the legal rights of the father over the child. It is interesting to note that the Criminal Code of Canada, Section 43, acknowledges the fact that:

> Every school teacher, parent or person standing in the place of a parent is justified in using force by way of correction towards a pupil or child, as the case may be, who is under his care, if the force does not exceed what is reasonable under the circumstances.[24]

This idea is also present in the civil law of Quebec.[25] The ideas reflected in these historical practices and beliefs still confuse present-day society which has not, as yet, clarified where cruelty of a mental and physical nature begins.

It was only one hundred years ago that the law began to recognize the child's rights as opposed to the rights of the parents to function as the sole authority over the child. This interference by the law in the traditional rights of the parents opened the door to protective legislation and society's involvement in the relationship between a parent and his child.

The first legal challenge to the absolute rights of parents over their children occurred in New York City in 1874. While visiting an aged woman in a tenement house, a church worker learned that a child named Mary Ellen was being inhumanly treated by her adoptive parents. This little girl was badly beaten daily. The child was also seriously malnourished and neglected. After appeals to protective agencies including the police and the district attorney's office proved useless, the woman, in desperation, appealed to Henry Bergh, a member of the American Society for the Prevention of Cruelty to Animals.

She pointed out that this child was being treated as an animal and was certainly a member of the animal kingdom. It was on this basis that the Society for the Prevention of Cruelty to Animals brought action which resulted in the child's removal from her parents.[26] One year later, in 1875 the New York Society for the Prevention of Cruelty to Children was organized. It is a sad commentary that it took the persistence of an unnamed church worker and the Society for the Prevention of Cruelty to Animals to instigate action in the first recorded case of a maltreated child.*[27]

Toronto was the first Canadian city to initiate a similar program when it established a Children's Aid Society in 1891. In 1893 the Ontario government was the first in Canada to pass legislation enabling Children's Aid Societies to be set up.[29] These societies, both in the United States and Canada, had only a small effect, however, on the incidence of child abuse. In 1892 the bodies of one hundred children were found in the streets of New York. When a pool on the campus of the University of Toronto was drained at the turn of the century, the bones of many newborn infants were discovered.[30]

Laws to protect children are very recent in the history of legislation, while child abuse in all its forms is a very old and terrible heritage of society. This information, however, should not give support to those who would dismiss action in this area on the grounds that one cannot legislate against an old evil.

For those who would abandon the child today on the basis of the horrendous historical evidence of child abuse, it should be remembered that the history of the slavery of children and adults alike is a long and terrible one, but that does not excuse or condone present-day practices. If we are to abandon the child on the assumption that nothing can be done because this has always gone on, or because child abuse is a part of human nature, we should apply the same argument to the conditions of the Indian, the Blacks, the poor, and even women, whose historical enslavement parallels in many ways the plight of children.[31]

Mistreatment of children is not a necessity resulting from our history. Rather, it reflects a continuation of our ignorance and our political, and hence legislative, impotency in the face of old customs and traditions.

*Even today "there are more contributors to the S.P.C.A. than to the Society to Prevent Cruelty to Children."[28]

Today the child, without being a proponent of any "ism," addresses the law and asks: "What is the difference between the system of formal slavery and the slavery of the family?" Surely it is time to examine the question that H. J. Nieboer and David B. Davis raise: Why has slavery historically been regarded as "the fact that one man is the property or possession of another *beyond* the limits of the family proper?"[32,33]

TYPICAL CASE PROFILE

AGE	three years
SEX	male
ASSAILANT	mother
RECENT EXTERNAL INJURIES	numerous bruises and abrasions, head, trunk, and extremities
REMOTE EXTERNAL INJURIES	numerous healing bruises, trunk, and extremities
FRACTURES	none
INTERNAL INJURIES	laceration, mesentery
CAUSE OF DEATH	laceration of mesentery with hemorrhage
PRESENTING STORY	"beat child"
METHOD OF INJURY	struck by hands
REASON FOR INJURY	"he needed love and attention"

EPILOGUE

If there are few statistics kept in Canada about the numbers of children who are actually maimed and murdered each year by parents, it stands to reason that there are no statistics about the numbers of children who are permanently brain-damaged as a result of battering. But the fact that there are no statistics does not change the reality of either of these tragedies. Unquestionably a large percentage of brain damage and retardation in children has resulted from blows which they have sustained.[1-3] Just as we understand, accept and portray in movies the punch-drunk fighter who has become addled and confused as a result of receiving too many blows to the head, so too do infants and children become damaged and confused and addled as a result of blows. The ear, eye and brain damage which is wantonly perpetrated on infants and children is beyond measure. The internal damage that is done to infants with blows to the kidneys, the spleen and the liver, and the scarring which is not seen, remains unrecorded. Even after a sad catalogue of misery such as the foregoing, the author has been asked the question, "Are you saying then, that we should never strike our children?" The answer has to be, "That is exactly what I am saying." Most parents will recall having in the heat of the moment hit a child harder than they had intended. The knowledge that it is very easy to innocently cause the child serious damage should persuade us that this form of discipline is far too dangerous to indulge in.

Institutions for cystic fibrosis and rare medical diseases happily bring forth from the community support in time and money, in addition to the substantial amounts invested in retarded children. However, this concern does not extend to the area of the battered child. The battered child is not only rejected by his parents, but rejected by Canadian society and the do-gooders of society. The child has also unquestionably been abandoned by the law. Legislators, judges and magistrates have failed to protect him. Again and again they return infants and small children to environments which send them back to hospitals with even more grave and terrible injuries than they originally received.

So much has been said about the role of the physician and his almost total negation of responsibility that it may seem tedious to repeat this point. Yet of all the professions which have, in effect, abandoned the battered child to his fate, the medical doctors are the most guilty of "seeing no evil," since to them the horrible facts of maltreatment are too terribly visible.

The practice of child battering continues unabated except for an occasional rumble of sympathy when an article in a magazine or newspaper exposes some hideous example. Immediately following there is a bit of an outcry. But afterward there is disinterest as people go back to the everyday business of their lives. The steps necessary to cope with, to prevent, and to cure the battering of children are relatively simple – far simpler than sending people to the moon, far simpler than putting a railroad from one end of Canada to the other, far simpler than many of the things which we have accomplished as a society. But it remains to be seen whether or not these steps will, in fact, be carried out.

In my submission to the Standing Committee on Health, Welfare and Social Affairs, I stated that we must look at the work done since the 1870s on the matter of the abuse of North American children. We have, all across North America, duplication of systems. We have competition between disciplines. We have no overall research design. We have no central funding. We have no universal protective plan, no universal treatment plan, no universal hospital or foster care plan. We have, in short, a failure to provide care or treatment for the child.

What is more, we have an attitude of hopelessness and despair at all levels of the community, in both the private and professional sectors. We also have a plethora of misinformation, myths, and empire-building. Further, we have a real reluctance to invest in the child the time and money necessary to create the kind of citizen we need if we are to survive tomorrow.

The child is a living system. It is not a single unit, but a system of units. Since Darwin, the study of human behaviour has increasingly been freed from censorship and prohibition. However, the study of human behaviour is still limited by taboos and customs.

In order to protect the child, protect the family, attend to the rights and protection of all the citizens of Canada, a full and co-ordinated overall approach to the problems of child abuse must be undertaken. The answer to the question, "Can we be successful?", lies in our attention to our goal – child protection.

I therefore submit the following points and proposals for consideration:

The history of child abuse is long. The law has closed its eyes to this abuse because it was the prerogative of citizens, under the law, to abuse their property as they saw fit. Wife, child, slave, and serf were all chattel, and as Aristotle has told us, one could do no injustice to one's own property.

Today, father, mother, state, and church still fight over the ownership of the child. If the abuse of children is to end, the law must cease to codify and protect these ownership rights.

The law, to be just, must stay the hand of the adult from striking the child. An assault is an assault. As the law protects adults from the assaults of others, the law must extend this protection to the child. The law must therefore delete Section 43 from the Canadian *Criminal Code*.

Unless the law can look with compassion on the child, no man or woman of compassion can call the law fair. Until the law accords the child the full protection of citizenship, the child will remain in its present condition. Citizenship is the birthright of the child and cannot continue to be withheld.

When the child attains such citizenship, the law need not protect the rights or reputation of the parents above the reputation and rights of the child. Too often the failure of physicians and others to report a parent who has most grievously injured a child has rested on the belief that one must not destroy the reputation of the parent by reporting the case. Physicians believe that they are treating the property of the parent, and therefore the person to be protected is the parent.

Surely the diagnosis of suspected child abuse dictates the treatment. Why deny a child treatment and protection because you might offend its parents unless old and strong precedents require such a procedure?

Citizenship in Canada confers the right to medical treatment by the state. Therefore the child as citizen must receive treatment unbiased by ownership. The child's medical record is a part of its medical treatment and protection, and therefore must be kept accurately.

If a child is a victim of abuse, this information is a vital part of its medical history. Therefore a full health record must be kept on every child from birth. This information, stored in a central computer, would be available to the medical attendants who must treat this child when it needs attention. A central health registry for all citizens in Canada is an important step in health care in a society that must cut health costs.

Thirty years ago Brock Chisholm, Deputy Minister of Health for Canada and Director General of the World Health Organization, told us if we wish to raise pigs successfully we should find out everything there is to know about pig-raising. He also told us if we want to raise children successfully we should find out everything there is to know about raising children. We would not treat or feed a pig in the manner we feed and treat children.

The effects of physical neglect range from complete starvation resulting in death, to chronic malnutrition. Physical neglect can also mean death due to filth and squalor of so horrendous a proportion that the mind recoils, to a chronic but mild disinterest in the health or safety of the child. The effects of emotional neglect range from death, to permanent derangement and brain damage.

Food and brains go together; smart is well fed, poorly fed is brain damaged. No sentimental statement about the poor child as genius will change the terrible tally of the countless poor children who are permanently stunted.

The law has historically hesitated to care for or feed a child because it did not wish to interfere with property rights. Yet the law cannot protect the citizen if it does not protect its life. Therefore, the law must provide for and nurture the life of the child. If the child is a citizen, then who feeds it is really a matter of delivery. The fact that it must eat is already assumed, even under its present legal status. What it eats and how often is now recognized as part of its rights under present health and welfare legislation. That new delivery systems should now be devised is only the implementation of these existing rights.

A physically or emotionally neglected child is a child of sick, ignorant or poor parents. Because a neglectful environment is a violation of a child's citizenship rights and is at present seen by law as a state problem, remedial programs are required.

Public health nursing units, day care and homemaker services are part of the answer to this delivery system. Failure to spend on these programs now is to spend later in the child's life, usually in a permanent fashion by long-term welfare or medical funding.

A child who is sexually molested is an abused child. The covert use of the bodies of children as sexual play things or piteous sexual victims is a part of adult pathology. The law must protect children from physical, emotional and sexual assaults on their persons and dignity. Sex education must be provided by law; parents can no longer be allowed to use children as sexual slaves. Ninety-eight per cent of sexually abused children are females.* The use of the tiny female's body for the pleasure of fathers, brothers, uncles, and neighbours must cease.

Sex education is one of the best protections the state can provide. Sex counselling is the best treatment the state can produce after the fact. Sexual understanding is the birthright of all citizens and prudish sentiment or religious myth will not pay the costs of injury and misery, or the money for the treatment of the law's failure to recognize that the child is a sexual human being.

*We have yet to reveal the true situation with regard to the sexual abuse of male children, but I suspect it is higher than we imagine.

133

A plan for preventing child abuse must not fool itself. Therefore, only a scientific approach will suffice.

To avoid the abuses of poor health, a child must be born of healthy stock and not inherit the ills of its breeding. (Brain-damaged children are at high risk.) All measures to have only healthy children should be made. Genetic counselling for parents is therefore essential.

To avoid the abuses of poor health, a child must receive an optimum diet during gestation. The care and feeding of the parent requires a completely healthy diet and environment.

To avoid the abuses of poor health, a child must be born in a safe and biologically proper fashion.

To avoid the abuses of mental illness (stress, frustration, fear, psychic shock, etc.), the child must be treated in a warm, receptive, and gentle fashion.

To avoid the abuses of nutritional, emotional, and physical deprivation, the child should be breast-fed for at least a year by an optimally fed, affectionate female.

To avoid the abuses of emotional neglect and intellectual impairment, a child must be held, cuddled, and engaged in emotional and physical dialogue.

To these ends I submit that:

1. The Parliament of Canada should invite the World Health Organization to advise and create, with medical and nursing associations, a home maternity system for training expectant mothers in nurturing, nutrition, and health care for children. Citizenship confers the right to health.

2. The Parliament of Canada should commission the World Federation for Mental Health to design a testing requirement for parenthood. We require people to be tested for driver's licences; we must not allow life to fall into the hands of those who, for whatever reasons, are not equipped to nurture it. Citizenship confers the right to protection.

3. The Parliament of Canada should undertake a complete standardized sex education curriculum for use at all levels of the community. Citizenship confers the right to know.

4. The Parliament of Canada should establish, as part of its federal health care program, a system to maintain full medical records for the treatment of citizens. A complete, on-going record, starting with prenatal exposure to drugs, anesthetics,

and x-rays, will protect the citizen from misuses of these treatments. Citizenship confers the right to correct treatment.

5. For the protection and treatment of citizens who are abused by their caretakers, a central treatment facility must be created by the Parliament of Canada.

Communication is the essential means of protection for the abused child. The telephone is therefore an important tool. Twenty-four hour telephone communication through one federal number should be provided all across Canada. By dialling the operator the reporting individual would be connected to a central intake headquarters. Highly-trained intake workers would receive these reports and then notify the proper provincial authorities.

6. The Parliament of Canada should move to create a federal Department of Youth to co-ordinate action on those problems that have a direct bearing on youth. In addition, this department would provide the necessary research and legal aid to all child citizens.

7. The mandate for legal action on behalf of the child citizen should remove or restrict the sale of products or articles unsafe for their use. An abused child is a child who is burned by inflammable fabric used for its pajamas. An abused child is also a child who has a violent allergic reaction to food additives arbitrarily placed in its food supply. Or a child who has been poisoned by lead, mercury, or asbestos inhalation placed in its life support system.

8. The child citizen cannot speak for itself. Citizenship confers the right to advocacy.

The vote of the child is for life. Given life by a power beyond the present comprehension of humanity, the child requires the compassion of the mature to sustain it. The system for feeding, protecting, and caring for children is well within the competence of life on this planet.

In order to protect the child, protect the family, attend to the rights and protection of all the citizens of Canada, a full and co-ordinated overall approach to the problems of child abuse must be undertaken. The answer to the question "Can we be successful?" lies in our attention to our goal – child protection.[4]

135

RECOMMENDATIONS AND COMMENTS FROM
BRIEFS AND EVIDENCE PRESENTED TO THE
HOUSE OF COMMONS STANDING COMMITTEE ON HEALTH,
WELFARE AND SOCIAL AFFAIRS
AND FROM DOCUMENTS TABLED WITH
THE COMMITTEE

Explanation of References in Appendix "A"

References taking the form of 31:22 identify the issue followed by the page number of the Minutes of Proceedings and Evidence of the Standing Committee on Health, Welfare and Social Affairs, First Session, Thirtieth Parliament, 1974-75-76.

1. EXCERPT FROM BRIEF PRESENTED BY THE DEPARTMENT OF JUSTICE

LEGAL FRAMEWORK FOR CHILD ABUSE

A. FEDERAL LEGISLATION

1. Criminal Code: R.S.C. 1970, c. C-34
    Sec. 26. Every one who is authorized by law to use force is criminally responsible for any excess thereof according to the nature and quality of the act that constitutes the excess. 1953-54, c. 51, s. 26.

    Sec. 43. Every schoolteacher, parent or person standing in the place of a parent is justified in using force by way of correction toward a pupil or child, as the case may be, who is under his care, if the force does not exceed what is reasonable under the circumstances. 1953-54, c. 51, s. 43.

    Sec. 146. (1) Every male person who has sexual intercourse with a female person who

    (a) is not his wife, and
    (b) is under the age of fourteen years,

    whether or not he believes that she is fourteen years of age or more, is guilty of an indictable offence and is liable to imprisonment for life and to be whipped.

    (2) Every male person who has sexual intercourse with a female who

    (a) is not his wife,
    (b) is of previously chaste character, and
    (c) is fourteen years of age or more and is under the age of sixteen years,

    whether or not he believes that she is sixteen years of age or more, is guilty of an indictable offence and is liable to imprisonment for five years.

(3) Where an accused is charged with an offence under subsection (2), the court may find the accused not guilty if it is of opinion that the evidence does not show that, as between the accused and the female person, the accused is more to blame than the female person. 1953-54, c. 51, s. 138: 1959, c. 41, s. 9.

Sec. 166. Every one who, being the parent or guardian of a female person,

(a) procures her to have illicit sexual intercourse with a person other than the procurer, or

(b) orders, is party to, permits or knowingly receives the avails of, the defilement, seduction or prostitution of the female person, is guilty of an indictable offence and is liable to

(c) imprisonment for fourteen years, if the female person is under the age of fourteen years, or

(d) imprisonment for five years, if the female person is fourteen years of age or more. 1953-54, c. 51, s. 155.

Sec. 168. (1) Every one who, in the home of a child, participates in adultery or sexual immorality or indulges in habitual drunkenness or any other form of vice, and thereby endangers the morals of the child or renders the home an unfit place for the child to be in, is guilty of an indictable offence and is liable to imprisonment for two years.

(2) No proceedings for an offence under this section shall be commenced more than one year after the time when the offence was committed.

(3) For the purposes of this section, "child" means a person who is or appears to be under the age of eighteen years.

(4) No proceedings shall be commenced under subsection (1) without the consent of the Attorney General, unless they are instituted by or at the instance of a recognized society for the protection of children or by an officer of a juvenile court. 1953-54, c.51, s.157.

Sec. 196. In this Part

"abandon" or "expose" includes

(a) a wilful omission to take charge of a child by a person who is under a legal duty to do so, and

(b) dealing with a child in a manner that is likely to leave that child exposed to risk without protection;

"child" includes an adopted child and an illegitimate child;

"form of marriage" includes a ceremony of marriage that is recognized as valid

(a) by the law of the place where it was celebrated, or

(b) by the law of the place where an accused is tried, notwithstanding that it is not recognized as valid by the law of the place where it was celebrated;

"guardian" includes a person who has in law or in fact the custody or control of a child. 1953-54, c.51, s.185.

Sec. 197. (1) Every one is under a legal duty

(a) as a parent, foster parent, guardian or head of a family, to provide necessaries of life for a child under the age of sixteen years;

(b) as a husband, to provide necessaries of life for his wife; and

(c) to provide necessaries of life to a person under his charge if that person

(i) is unable, by reason of detention, age, illness, insanity or other cause, to withdraw himself from that charge, and

(ii) is unable to provide himself with necessaries of life.

(2) Every one commits an offence who, being under a legal duty within the meaning of subsection (1), fails without lawful excuse, the proof of which lies upon him, to perform that duty, if

(a) with respect to a duty imposed by paragraph (1)(a) or (b),

(i) the person to whom the duty is owed is in destitute or necessitous circumstances, or

(ii) the failure to perform the duty endangers the life of the person to whom the duty is owed, or causes or is likely to cause the health of that person to be endangered permanently; or

(b) with respect to a duty imposed by paragraph (1)(c), the failure to perform the duty endangers the life of the person to whom the duty is owed or causes or is likely to cause the health of that person to be injured permanently.

(3) Every one who commits an offence under subsection (2) is guilty of

(a) an indictable offence and is liable to imprisonment for two years; or

(b) an offence punishable on summary conviction.

(4) For the purpose of proceedings under this section,

(a) evidence that a man has cohabited with a woman or has in any way recognized her as being his wife is, in the absence of any evidence to the contrary, proof that they are lawfully married;

(b) evidence that a person has in any way recognized a child as being his child is prima facie proof that the child is his child;

(c) evidence that a man has left his wife and has failed, for a period of any one month subsequent to the time of his so leaving, to make provision for her maintenance or for the maintenance of any child of his under the age of sixteen years, is prima facie proof that he has failed without lawful excuse to provide necessaries of life for them; and

(d) the fact that a wife or child is receiving or has received necessaries of life from another person who is not under a legal duty to provide them is not a defence. 1953-54, c.51, s.186; 1968-69, c.38, s.92.

Sec. 200. Every one who unlawfully abandons or exposes a child who is under the age of ten years, so that its life is or is likely to be endangered or its health is or is likely to be permanently injured, is guilty of an indictable offence and is liable to imprisonment for two years. 1953-54, c.51, s.189.

Sec. 205. (1) A person commits homicide when, directly or indirectly, by any means, he causes the death of a human being.

(2) Homicide is culpable or not culpable.

(3) Homicide that is not culpable is not an offence.

(4) Culpable homicide is murder or manslaughter or infanticide.

(5) A person commits culpable homicide when he causes the death of a human being,

(a) by means of an unlawful act,

(b) by criminal negligence,

(c) by causing that human being, by threats or fear of violence or by deception, to do anything that causes his death, or

(d) by wilfully frightening that being, in the case of a child or sick person.

Sec. 206. (1) A child becomes a human being within the meaning of this Act when it has completely proceeded, in a living state, from the body of its mother whether or not

(a) it has breathed,

(b) it has an independent circulation, or

(c) the navel string is severed.

(2) A person commits homicide when he causes injury to a child before or during its birth as a result of which the child dies after becoming a human being. 1953-54, c. 51, s. 195; 1968-69, c. 38, s. 14.

Sec. 216. A female person commits infanticide when by a wilful act or omission she causes the death of her newly-born child, if at the time of the act or omission she is not fully recovered from the effects of giving birth to the child and by reason thereof or of the effect of lactation consequent on the birth of the child her mind is then disturbed. 1953-54, c. 51, s. 204.

Sec. 244. A person commits an assault when, without the consent of another person or with consent, where it is obtained by fraud,

(a) he applies force intentionally to the person of the other, directly or indirectly, or

(b) he attempts or threatens, by an act or gesture, to apply force to the person of the other, if he has or causes the other to believe upon reasonable grounds that he has present ability to effect his purpose. 1953-54, c. 51, s. 230.

Sec. 245. (1) Every one who commits a common assault is guilty of an offence punishable on summary conviction.

(2) Every one who unlawfully causes bodily harm to any person or commits an assault that causes bodily harm to any person is guilty of an indictable offence and is liable to imprisonment for five years. 1953-54, c. 51, s. 231; 1972, c. 13, s. 21.

Sec. 246 (1) Every one who assaults a person with intent to commit an indictable offence is guilty of an indictable offence and is liable to imprisonment for five years.

2. *Canada Evidence Act,* R.S.C. 1970, c. E-10.

Sec. 4. (1) Every person charged with an offence, and, except as otherwise provided in this section, the wife or husband, as the case may be, of the person so charged, is a competent witness for the defence, whether the person so charged is charged solely or jointly with any other person.

(2) The wife or husband of a person charged with an offence against section 33 or 34 of the Juvenile Delinquents Act or with an offence against any of sections 143 to 146, 148, 150 to 155, 157, 166 to 169, 175, 195, 197, 200, 248 to 250, 255 to 258, 289, paragraph 423(1)(c) or an attempt to commit an offence under section 146 or 155 of the Criminal Code, is a competent and compellable witness for the prosecution without the consent of the person charged.

(3) No husband is compellable to disclose any communication made to him by his wife during their marriage, and no wife is compellable to disclose any communication made to her by her husband during their marriage.

(4) Nothing in this section affects a case where the wife or husband of a person charged with an offence may at common law be called as a witness without the consent of that person.

(5) The failure of the person charged, or of the wife or husband of such person, to testify, shall not be made the subject of comment by the judge, or by counsel for the prosecution. R.S., c. 307, s. 4; 1953-54, c. 51, s. 749.

Sec. 16. (1) In any legal proceeding where a child of tender years is offered as a witness, and such child does not, in the opinion of the judge, justice or other presiding officer, understand the nature of an oath, the evidence of such child may be received, though not given upon oath, if, in the opinion of the judge, justice or other presiding officer, as the case may be, the child is possessed of sufficient intelligence to justify the reception of the evidence, and understands the duty of speaking the truth.

(2) No case shall be decided upon such evidence alone, and it must be corroborated by some other material evidence. R.S., c. 307, s. 16.

...

4. Present Case Handling Practices

At the present time, most child abuse cases are handled out of court or appear in family courts as cases of neglect or "children in need or protection" under provincial child welfare legislation for a number of reasons.

(a) As understanding of the causes of child abuse has increased, there has been a shift of emphasis from rescue of the child and punishment of the parent toward the treatment and care of both parents and children with prosecution seen by provincial authorities as appropriate in a limited number of cases.

(b) Criminal Code prosecutions are normally expensive and time consuming procedures during which a child may be left in legal limbo.

(c) Evidentiary rules and the standards of proof required are factors.

(i) Criminal convictions are difficult to obtain because it must be established beyond a reasonable doubt that a particular person assaulted the child. Abuse of children generally takes place in the privacy of the home in the absence of witnesses who will or can testify. Normally the only witnesses to the abuse are the other members of the family – that is the other parent and any other children. Under existing evidence rules, if the parents or adults of the household are not legally married, the law considers them strangers for purposes of criminal proceedings and the prosecution can compel one to testify against the other. If the parents are married, the spouse not charged is neither compellable nor competent to give evidence for the prosecution even if he or she were willing to do so unless the offence is one of a number of specified exempted offences and a non-sexual assault on a child is not one such offence. As for the victim himself and the other children, a "child of tender years" may give evidence, although he or she is unable to understand the nature of an oath, only if "the child is possessed of sufficient intelligence to justify the reception of the evidence and understands the duty of speaking the truth". In addition, no case shall be decided upon such unsworn evidence alone and must be corroborated by some other material evidence which may be a difficult evidentiary requirement to satisfy. Furthermore the recollection of events and the credibility of the other children in the family may be reduced if, while the alleged victim of abuse may have been removed to a place of safety soon after the alleged incident, the other children who are capable of serving as witnesses remain with the parents prior to the criminal proceedings.

(ii) On the other hand, neglect proceedings are civil proceedings so the neglect or need for protection need only be established by the balance of probabilities or a preponderance of evidence. In addition, American and Canadian judges have begun to borrow from the evidentiary law of negligence the principle of "res ipsa loquitur" and have held that the condition of the child speaks for itself. They have thus permitted an inference of negligence to be drawn from proof of the child's age and the number and nature of the child's injuries and from the fact that the child's condition is such as in the ordinary course of things does not happen if the caretaker who has the responsibility and control of the child has used proper care. In Ontario for example, a child in need of protection includes a child who is living in an unfit and improper place. If a child suffers injuries which cannot be explained satisfactorily by the caretaker of the child, it is presumed from the condition of the child itself that the child is living in an unfit and improper place.

(d) Family counselling as well as protective supervision can be ordered for the child and his or her family under provincial child welfare legislation. One's parenting skills are unlikely to improve solely because of a criminal conviction and sentence and, in addition, even if the abuser is convicted and incarcerated, he or she will probably eventually return to live with the non-charged spouse in whose care the victim may have been during the incarceration and the family must be taught to function better as a unit if abusive behaviour is not to be repeated.[1]

APPENDIX B

DEFINITIONS OF "NEGLECTED CHILDREN" CONTAINED IN PROVINCIAL STATUTES

Newfoundland: The Child Welfare Act
2. In this Act,
   (a) "child" means an unmarried boy or girl actually or apparently under the age of sixteen years.

. . .

(p) "neglected child" means

    (i) a child who is without proper supervision or control,

    (ii) a child who is living in circumstances that are unfit or improper for the child,

    (iii) a child in the care or custody of a person who is unfit, unable or unwilling to exercise proper care over the child,

    (iv) a child whose life, health, or emotional welfare is endangered,

    (v) a child who is in the care and custody of a person

        (A) who fails to provide for his education, or

        (B) who does not try to prevent habitual absences of the child from school when there is no valid reason for the absence,

    (vi) a child in respect of whom an offence has been committed under subsection (4) or (5) of section 4 of *The Adoption of Children Act, 1972*, or under an equivalent statutory provision in force before that Act,

    (vii) a child who has no living parents and who has no person willing to assume responsibility or with a legal responsibility for his maintenance,

    (viii) a child who is in the care or custody of a person who refuses or fails

        (A) to provide or obtain proper medical or other recognized remedial care or treatment necessary for the health or well-being of the child, or

        (B) to permit such care and treatment to be supplied to the child when it is considered essential by a duly qualified medical practitioner.

Prince Edward Island: The Children's Protection Act

1. In this Act,

    . . .

(c) "child" means a boy or girl actually or apparently under the age of seventeen years;

    . . .

(1) "neglected child" means

    (i) a child who is found

        (A) begging or receiving alms,

        (B) thieving in any place whatsoever, or

        (C) loitering in or near a public place after nine o'clock in the evening, not accompanied by his parent or guardian, or by some adult person with the consent of the parent or guardian,

    (ii) a child who is found wandering about at late hours and not having any home or settled place of abode or proper guardianship;

    (iii) a child who is found sleeping at night in other than proper housing accommodations or without proper adult supervision;

    (iv) a child who is found associating or dwelling with a thief, drunkard, vagrant, prostitute, dissolute or vicious person, or frequenting a house of ill-fame;

    (v) a child who is growing up without salutary parental control and education or in circumstances tending to make him idle, dissolute, delinquent or incorrigible;

    (vi) a child whose environment is or is likely to become injurious to his health or well-being by reason of deprivation, ill treatment or personal injury or because of the habitual intemperance, marital discord or grave misconduct of his parents or either of them;

(vii) a child whose home by reason of neglect, cruelty, immorality, disease or unsanitary conditions is an unfit or improper place for the child, or who has not proper guardianship or who has no parent capable of exercising proper parental control;

(viii) a child who is an orphan and who is not being properly cared for, or who is brought, with the consent of the person in whose charge he is before a judge to be dealt with under this Act;

(ix) a child who without sufficient cause, habitually absents himself from his home or school;

(x) a child whose parent or guardian neglects or refuses to provide or secure proper medical, surgical or other remedial care or treatment necessary for his health or well-being, or who refuses to permit such treatment to be supplied to the child when it is recommended by a duly qualified medical practitioner;

(xi) a child who is abandoned or deserted by his parents or only living parent, or who is deserted by one parent and whose other parent fails to properly care for him;

(xii) a child whose parent wishes to divest himself of his responsibilities toward the child;

(xiii) a child who habitually uses obscene, profane or indecent language or is guilty of immoral conduct in any place whatsoever;

(xiv) a child whose life, health or morals may be endangered by the conduct of the person in whose charge he is.

Nova Scotia: Children's Services Act

1. In this Act,

(i) "child" means a boy or girl under sixteen years of age, unless the context otherwise requires;
. . .

(m) "child in need of protection" means

(i) a child who is without proper supervision or control,

(ii) a child who is living in circumstances that are unfit or improper for the child,

(iii) a child in the care or custody of a person who is unfit, unable or unwilling to exercise proper care over the child,

(iv) a child whose life, health or emotional welfare is endangered,

(v) a child who is in the care or custody of a person who fails to provide for his education,

(vi) a child who is committed pursuant to paragraph (h) or (i) of subsection (1) of Section 20 of the Juvenile Delinquents Act (Canada), or

(vii) a child who is in the care or custody of a person who refuses or fails

(A) to provide or obtain proper medical or other recognized remedial care or treatment necessary for the health or well-being of the child, or

(B) to permit such care and treatment to be supplied to the child when it is considered essential by a duly qualified medical practitioner.

New Brunswick: Child Welfare Act

1. In this Act,

   ...

      (b) "child" means a boy or girl actually or apparently under sixteen years of age;

      ...

7. An officer may, without a warrant, apprehend and detain as a child in need of protection, a child

      (a) whose life, health, or morals may be endangered by the conduct of his parent;

      (b) who is found not properly cared for by his parent;

      (c) who has been assaulted or ill-used by his parent;

      (d) who is deserted by his parent;

      (e) who is tending to become incorrigible, dissolute or delinquent by reason of inadequate control by his parent;

      (f) whose parent neglects or refuses to provide, secure or permit proper medical, surgical or other remedial care or treatment necessary for his health or well-being;

      (g) who is emotionally rejected or deprived of affection by his parent sufficient to endanger his emotional and mental development, and such condition is supported in writing by a psychiatrist who is duly registered in the Register of the Medical Council of New Brunswick and licensed to practice and in good standing;

      (h) who is found under circumstances indicating that he has no home or settled place of abode or proper guardianship;

      (i) who is living in an unfit place;

      (j) who is found associating with an improper person;

      (k) who conducts himself immorally;

      (l) who, without sufficient cause, habitually absents himself from his home or school, or whose parent or teacher represents that he is beyond control;

      (m) who commits an offence punishable by fine or imprisonment or both;

      (n) who is born of parents not married to each other whose mother is unable, unfit or unwilling to care properly for him;

      (o) who is under the age of twelve years and is left without the care or supervision of a person over the age of twelve years.

Quebec: Youth Protection Act

1. In this Act the following terms mean

      ...

      (f) "child": a boy or a girl apparently or effectively aged less than eighteen years;

      ...

15.(1) When a child is particularly exposed to moral or physical dangers, by reason of its environment or other special circumstances, and for such reasons needs to be protected, any person in authority may bring him or have him brought before a judge. A judge may also, upon information which he deems serious, to the effect that a child is in the above described conditions, order that he be brought before him.

Without limiting the generality of the provisions of the preceding paragraph, children whose parents, tutors or guardians are deemed unworthy, orphans with neither father nor mother and cared for by nobody, abandoned, illegitimate or adulterine children, those particularly exposed to delinquency by their environment, unmanageable children generally showing pre-delinquency traits, as well as those exhibiting serious character disturbances, may be considered as being in the conditions contemplated by the preceding paragraph.

Ontario: The Child Welfare Act (Part II)

20. (1) In this Part

   (a) "child" means a boy or girl actually or apparently under sixteen years of age;

   (b) "Child in need of protection" means,

      (i) a child who is brought, with the consent of the person in whose charge he is, before a judge to be dealt with under this Part;

      (ii) a child who is deserted by the person in whose charge he is;

      (iii) a child where the person in whose charge he is cannot for any reason care properly for him, or where that person has died and there is no suitable person to care for the child;

      (iv) a child who is living in an unfit or improper place;

      (v) a child found associating with an unfit or improper person;

      (vi) a child found begging or receiving alms in a public place;

      (vii) Repealed.

      (viii) a child whose parent is unable to control him;

      (ix) a child who, without sufficient cause, habitually absents himself from his home or school;

      (x) a child where the person in whose charge he is neglects or refuses to provide or obtain proper medical, surgical or other recognized remedial care or treatment necessary for his health or well-being, or refuses to permit such care or treatment to be supplied to the child when it is recommended by a legally qualified medical practitioner, or otherwise fails to protect the child adequately;

      (xi) a child whose emotional or mental development is endangered because of emotional rejection or deprivation of affection by the person in whose charge he is;

      (xii) a child whose life, health or morals may be endangered by the conduct of the person in whose charge he is;

Manitoba: The Child Welfare Act

1. In this Act

   . . .

   (b) "child" means a person under the age of majority.

   . . .

   Child in need of protective guardianship.

16. In this Act, a child in need of protective guardianship means

   (a) a child who is an orphan or who has been abandoned or deserted by his parents and

      (i) who is not being properly cared for by anyone, or

      (ii) who with the consent of the person in whose charge he is, is brought before a judge to be dealt with under this Act;

(b) a child where the parent or person in whose charge he is cannot, by reason of disease, infirmity, misfortune, incompetence, imprisonment, or any combination thereof, care properly for him;

(c) a child whose life, physical or mental health, or morals may be endangered by the conduct of the person in whose charge he is;

(d) a child who is beyond the control of his parents or person in whose charge he is;

(e) a child whose behaviour, condition, environment or association is injurious to himself or others;

(f) a child born to parents not married to each other whose mother is unable or unwilling to care for him; or

(g) a child where the parent or person in whose charge he is neglects or refuses to provide or obtain proper medical, surgical, or other remedial care or treatment necessary for health and well-being of the child, or refuses to permit such care or treatment to be supplied to the child when it is recommended by a duly qualified medical practitioner.

Saskatchewan: The Family Services Act

2. In this Act:

(a) "child" means a boy or girl actually or apparently under the age of sixteen years.

. . .

15. A child is in need of protection when:

(a) he is without proper or competent supervision;

(b) he is living in circumstances that are unfit or improper for him;

(c) he is in the custody of a person who is unable or unwilling to exercise proper control over the child;

(d) his life, health or emotional welfare is endangered by the conduct of the person who has custody of the child;

(e) the person in whose custody he is neglects or refuses to provide or obtain proper medical, surgical or other recognized remedial care or treatment necessary for his health or well-being or normal development, or refuses to permit such care or treatment to be supplied to the child when it is considered essential by a duly qualified medical practitioner;

(f) his parent is unfit, unable or unwilling to care for him.

Alberta: The Child Welfare Act

14. In this Part (i.e. Part 2),

(a) "child" means a boy or girl actually or apparently under eighteen years of age.

. . .

(e) "neglected child" means a child in need of protection and without restricting the generality of the foregoing includes any child who is within one or more of the following descriptions:

(i) a child who is not being properly cared for;

(ii) a child who is abandoned or deserted by the person in whose charge he is or who is an orphan who is not being properly cared for;

(iii) a child where the person in whose charge he is cannot, by reason of disease or infirmity or misfortune or incompetence or imprisonment or any combination thereof, care properly for him;

(iv) a child who is living in an unfit or improper place;

(v) a child found associating with an unfit or improper person;

(vi) a child found begging in a public place;

(vii) a child who, with the consent or connivance of the person in whose charge he is, commits any act that renders him liable to a penalty under any Act of the Parliament of Canada or of the Legislature, or under any municipal by-law;

(viii) a child who is misdemeanant by reason of the inadequacy of the control exercised by the person in whose charge he is, or who is being allowed to grow up without salutary parental control or under circumstances tending to make him idle or dissolute;

(ix) a child who, without sufficient cause, habitually absents himself from his home or school;

(x) a child where the person in whose charge he is neglects or refuses to provide or obtain proper medical, surgical or other remedial care or treatment necessary for his health or well-being, or refuses to permit such care or treatment to be supplied to the child when it is recommended by a duly qualified medical practitioner;

(xi) a child whose emotional or mental development is endangered because of emotional rejection or deprivation of affection by the person in whose charge he is;

(xii) a child whose life, health or morals may be endangered by the conduct of the person in whose charge he is;

(xiii) a child who is being cared for by and at the expense of someone other than his parents and in circumstances which indicate that his parents are not performing their parental duties toward him;

(xiv) a child who is not under proper guardianship or who has no parent

   (A) capable of exercising, or
   (B) willing to exercise, or
   (C) capable of exercising and willing to exercise, proper parental control over the child;

(xv) a child whose parent wishes to divest himself of his parental responsibilities toward the child.

British Columbia: Protection of Children Act

7. (1) The Superintendent and every person who is authorized in writing by the Superintendent, every constable or officer of the Provincial police or of any municipal police, and every Probation Officer, may apprehend, without warrant, and bring before a Judge, as needing protection, any child apparently under the age of seventeen years who is within any of the following classes or descriptions: –

(a) Who is found begging in any street, house, or place of public resort, whether actually begging or under pretext of selling or offering anything for sale;

(b) Who is found sleeping at night in other than proper housing accommodation and without proper adult supervision;

(c) Who is found associating or dwelling with a thief, drunkard, or vagrant, or who, by reason of neglect or drunkenness or other vices of the parents or guardians, is suffered to grow up without salutary parental control and education, or in circumstances exposing such child to an idle or dissolute life;

(d) Who is found in any disorderly house, or in company of people reputed to be criminal, immoral, or disorderly;

(e) Who is an orphan without adequate protection for his upbringing;

(f) Who has been deserted by his parents;

(g) Who is found guilty of petty crimes, and who is likely to develop criminal tendencies if not removed from his surroundings;

(h) Who is found wandering about at late hours and not having any home or settled place of abode or proper guardianship;

(i) (Repealed)

(j) Whose only parent or whose parents are undergoing imprisonment;

(k) Whose home by reason of neglect, cruelty, or depravity is an unfit place for the child, or who has no proper guardianship, or whose parent or parents are unfit, unable, or unwilling to care properly for him;

(l) Who is subject to such blindness, deafness, feeble-mindedness, or physical disability as is likely to make him a charge upon the public, or who is exposed to infection from tuberculosis or from any venereal disease where proper precautions to prevent infection are not taken, or who is suffering from such a lack of medical or surgical care as is likely to interfere with his normal development;

(m) Who, by reason of the action of his parents or otherwise, is habitually truant from school and is liable to grow up without proper education;

(n) Who is neglected so as to be in a state of habitual vagrancy or mendicancy;

(o) Who is ill-treated so as to be in peril in respect of life, health, or morality by continued personal injury, or by grave misconduct or habitual intemperance of the parents.

Northwest Territories: Child Welfare Ordinance

2. (b) "child" means a person actually or apparently under the age of sixteen years, . . .

. . .

13. (1) For the purposes of this Part a child is deemed to be in need of protection when

(a) he is an orphan who is not being properly cared for or is brought, with the consent of the person in whose charge he is, before a justice to be dealt with under this Part;

(ab) he has been born out of wedlock and his mother has delivered him to the Superintendent for adoption;

(b) he is deserted by the person in whose charge he is, or that person has died or is unable to care properly for him;

(c) the person in whose charge he is cannot, by reason of disease, infirmity, misfortune, incompetence, imprisonment or any combination thereof, care properly for him;

(d) his home, by reason of neglect, cruelty or depravity on the part of the person in whose charge he is, is an unfit and improper place for him;

(e) he is found associating with an unfit or improper person;

(f) he is found begging in a public place;

(g) with the consent or connivance of the person in whose charge he is, he commits any act that renders him liable to a penalty under any Ordinance, Act of the Parliament of Canada or municipal by-law;

(h) he is delinquent or incorrigible by reason of the inadequacy of the control exercised by the person in whose charge he is, or he is being allowed to grow up under circumstances tending to make him dissolute;

(i) he habitually absents himself from the home of the person in whose charge he is without sufficient cause;

(j) the person in whose charge he is neglects or refuses to provide or secure proper medical, surgical or other remedial care or treatment necessary for his health or well-being, or refuses to permit such care or treatment to be supplied to the child when it is recommended by a duly qualified medical practitioner; or

(k) he is deprived of affection by the person in whose charge he is to a degree that, on the evidence of a psychiatrist, is sufficient to endanger his emotional and mental development.

Yukon: Child Welfare Ordinance

2. (c) "child" means an unmarried person

      (i) actually or apparently under the age of eighteen

       . . .

6. For the purpose of this Part a child is deemed to be in need of protection when

(a) he is an orphan who is not being properly cared for;

(b) he is deserted by the person in whose charge he is;

(c) the person in whose charge he is cannot care properly for him;

(d) he is brought, with the consent of the person in whose charge he is, before a justice to be dealt with under this Part;

(e) he is under the age of twelve years and is frequently left by the person in whose charge he is without care and supervision of an older person or when such older person fails to give him proper and adequate care and supervision;

(f) his home, by reason of neglect or depravity on the part of the person in whose charge he is, is an unfit or improper place for him;

(g) he is found associating with an unfit or improper person who is not his parent;

(h) he is found begging in any street, house or place of public resort, whether actually begging or under the pretext of selling or offering anything for sale or is found loitering in a public place;

(i) with the consent or connivance of the person in whose charge he is, he commits any act that renders him liable to a penalty under any ordinance, Act of Parliament of Canada or municipal by-law;

(j) by reason of the inadequacy of the control exercised by the person in whose charge he is, he is being allowed to grow up under circumstances tending to make him idle, dissolute, delinquent or incorrigible, or without a proper education;

(k) he habitually absents himself from the home of the person in whose charge he is, or from school when he is within the compulsory school attendance age, without sufficient cause;

(l) the person in whose charge he is neglects or refuses to provide or secure proper medical, surgical or other remedial care or treatment for his health or well-being, or refuses to permit such care or treatment to be supplied to the child when it is recommended by a medical practitioner;

(m) he is deprived of affection by the person in whose charge he is to a degree that is sufficient to hinder his emotional and mental develoment;

(n) he is by reason of the ill-treatment, cruelty, frequent personal injury, grave misconduct or frequent intemperance of or by the person in whose charge he is, in danger of loss of life, health or morality;

(o) the person in whose charge he is, is incapable of exercising or unwilling to exercise proper parental control;

(p) he is a child born out of wedlock whose mother consents to him being brought before a justice for the purpose of transferring his guardianship to the Director;

(q) his parents or only parent is undergoing imprisonment or is a patient in a hospital for the mentally ill, a tuberculosis sanatorium, or rehabilitation centre for physical restoration of the disabled.[2]

APPENDIX C

MANDATORY REPORTING PROVISIONS IN PROVINCIAL CHILD WELFARE LEGISLATION

Nine jurisdictions – eight provinces (Nfld., N.S., Quebec, Ontario, Manitoba, Saskatchewan, Alberta, B.C.) and the Yukon Territory now make it mandatory under their child welfare legislation for a person having knowledge of the ill-treatment of a child to report the facts as he knows them to the child welfare authority.

These provisions have been introduced since 1965 in the following order of the initial reporting requirement:

1965	Ontario
1966	Alberta
1967	British Columbia
1968	Nova Scotia
1969	Newfoundland
1970	Manitoba
1970	Yukon
1973	Saskatchewan
1974	Quebec

The reporting requirements cover such matters as the abandonment, desertion, physical ill-treatment or need for protection of a child. All jurisdictions protect the informant against any action, unless the report has been made with malicious intent or without reasonable and probable grounds for belief.

Four of the jurisdictions (Ontario, Manitoba, Saskatchewan, and B.C.) have no penalty for failure to report such incidents. Although Alberta has a provision for penalty, this subsection has not been proclaimed. The Yukon Territory has specific penalties for failure to report child abuse. In three other provinces – Newfoundland, Quebec and Nova Scotia – the general provisions for violation of the Act apply.

The following are excerpts from provincial legislation requiring the reporting of child abuse.

Newfoundland: The Child Welfare (Amendment) Act, 1969

49 (1) Every person having information of the abandonment, desertion, physical ill-treatment or need for protection of a child shall report the information to the Director or welfare officer.

(2) Subsection (1) applies notwithstanding that the information is confidential or privileged, and no action lies against the informant unless the giving of the information is done maliciously or without reasonable and probable cause.

(3) Any person who fails to comply with or otherwise contravenes any of the provisions of this section is guilty of an offence.

(The penalty for a breach of any provision of the Act on summary conviction is a fine not exceeding $200, or in default of payment, imprisonment for a term not exceeding 2 months or both.)

Nova Scotia: Children's Services Act

77 (1) Every person having information, whether confidential or privileged, of the need for protection of a child shall report the information to an agency.

(2) No action lies against a person who gives information under subsection (1) unless the giving of the information is done maliciously or without reasonable and probable cause.

(3) Any person who knowingly or willfully by any act or omission or failure to report thereby causing, producing, promoting or contributing to a child being or likely to become a child in need of protection shall be guilty of an offence under this Act.

(There is no specific penalty for violation of this provision, but a general penalty applies. Any person who violates any provision of the Act or the regulations is liable, unless a penalty is provided elsewhere in the Act, to a fine of not more than one thousand dollars or to imprisonment for not more than one year, or both.)

42 The Minister shall establish a child abuse register.

43 (1) Where

(a) a child is a child in need of protection within the meaning of subclause (iv) or (vii) of clause (m) of Section 2; or

(b) a qualified medical practitioner, registered nurse, or administrator of a hospital or institution reports that he has reasonable and probable grounds to believe a child is subject to child abuse,

it shall be recorded in the child abuse register and the person purported to have abused the child shall be informed of such recording as soon as practicable.

(2) The child abuse register shall be treated as confidential and shall be available only upon the approval of the Administrator for the purposes of

(a) research as defined by regulations; or

(b) assisting in the study of the circumstances where a child is suspected to be in need of protection.

Quebec: The Youth Protection Act as amended in 1974 by an Act Respecting the Protection of Children Subject to Ill-treatment

14j. Every person, even one having privileged information by reason of his office, who has reasonable cause to believe that a child is subject to physical ill-treatment as the result of abuse or neglect is bound to bring the situation to the attention of the committee without delay.

Failure to observe the preceding paragraph is an offence under this act.

14k. No civil action may be instituted on the grounds that a person has, in good faith, brought a situation contemplated in section 14j to the attention of the committee.

(No specific penalty is prescribed but failure to report this information is an offence under the Act. The penalty on summary conviction for neglecting to protect a child from moral or physical danger is a fine of not more than $300 or imprisonment of not more than one year, or both.)

Ontario : The Child Welfare Act, 1965

41 (1) Every person having information of the abandonment, desertion, physical ill-treatment or need for protection of a child shall report the information to a children's aid society or Crown Attorney.

(2) Subsection (1) applies notwithstanding that the information is confidential or privileged, and no action shall be instituted against the informant unless the giving of the information is done maliciously or without reasonable and probable cause.

(No provision for penalty.)

Manitoba: The Child Welfare Act 1974

36 (1) Every person having information of the abandonment, desertion, ill-treatment or need for protection of a child shall report the information to the director or to a child caring agency.

(2) Subsection (1) applies notwithstanding that the information is confidential or privileged; and no action lies against the informant for reporting the information unless it is reported maliciously or without reasonable and probable cause.

(No provision for penalty.)

Saskatchewan: The Family Services Act, 1973

16 (1) Every person having information that a child is in need of protection shall report the information to an officer or peace officer.

(2) A person who makes a report pursuant to subsection (1) is not liable in any action for making the report unless the report is false and is made maliciously.

(3) Every peace officer who is in receipt of information that a child is in need of protection shall forthwith report the information to an officer of the department.

(4) The department shall investigate reports or complaints of neglect, abuse, exploitation or cruel treatment of a child and provide such services to any person as may be necessary to reduce or eliminate any neglect, abuse, exploitation or cruel treatment found to exist.

(No provision for penalty.)

Alberta: The Child Welfare Amendment Act, 1973

41(1) Any person who has reasonable and probable ground to believe and believes that a child has been abandoned, deserted, physically ill-treated or is in need of protection shall forthwith report the ground of such belief to the Director or to any child welfare worker of the Department.

(2) Subsection (1) applies notwithstanding that the ground for belief is

information that is confidential or privileged, and no action lies against the person so reporting unless the provision of the report is done maliciously or without reasonable and probable ground for belief.

(3) Any person who fails to comply with subsection (1) in addition to any civil liability, is guilty of an offence and liable upon summary conviction to a fine of not more than $500 and in default of payment to imprisonment for a term not exceeding six months or to both fine and imprisonment. (Not proclaimed)

41.1 The Director shall maintain a registry for the purpose of recording all reports received under section 41.

41.2 Upon a report being made pursuant to section 41, the Director shall cause the report to be examined and shall direct such further investigations of the matter reported as he considers necessary.

(The penalty for failing to report a condition of physical ill-treatment of a child on summary conviction is a fine of not more than $500 and in default of payment, imprisonment for a term not exceeding 6 months or both.)

British Columbia: Protection of Children Act Amendment Act, 1974

7 (2) Every person who has reasonable grounds for suspecting that a child

(a) has been or is being abandoned, deserted, or maltreated; or

(b) is otherwise in need of protection,

shall, notwithstanding any claim of confidentiality or privilege that may exist or be made,

(c) forthwith make a complete report of the circumstances to the Superintendent; and

(d) where subpoenaed and called to give evidence in a proceeding, give such evidence of the circumstances as the court may require.

(3) Where a family advocate appointed under the Unified Family Court Act suspects that a child

(a) has been or is being abandoned, deserted, or maltreated; or

(b) is otherwise in need of protection,

he may request any person who he believes has information relevant to the matter to make a complete report of the information to him and on the receipt of the request of the family advocate, the person shall forthwith make the report.

(4) The Superintendent and the family advocate are entitled, on request, to a copy of any report made under subsections (2) or (3).

(5) No person is liable for any loss or damage suffered by any person by reason only of making or providing, in good faith, a report under subsection (2), (3), or (4).

(No provision for penalty.)

Yukon: Child Welfare Ordinance, 1970

25(1) Every person having information of the abandonment, desertion, physical ill-treatment or need for protection of a child shall report the information to the Director, the Assistant Director or any member of the social work staff of the Department of Social Welfare.

(2) Subsection (1) applies notwithstanding that the information is confidential or privileged, and no action lies against the informant unless the giving of the information is done maliciously or without reasonable and probable cause.

(The penalty for violation of this provision on summary conviction is a fine not exceeding $500 or imprisonment for a term not exceeding 6 months, or both fine and imprisonment.)[3]

APPENDIX D

PENALTIES PROVIDED IN PROVINCIAL CHILD WELFARE LEGISLATION RELATING SPECIFICALLY TO THE ABUSE OF CHILDREN

Newfoundland: The Child Welfare Act

34. (1) Subject to subsection (3), any person who

. . .

> (c) wilfully commits or omits an act producing, promoting or contributing to a child being or becoming a neglected child, is guilty of an offence and liable on summary conviction to a fine not exceeding two hundred dollars or, in default of payment, to imprisonment for a term not exceeding two months, or to both such fine and such imprisonment.

Prince Edward Island: The Children's Protection Act

27. Any person who, having the care, custody, control or charge of a child under the age of eighteen years, ill-treats, neglects, deserts, or abandons or exposes the child, or causes or procures the child to be ill-treated, neglected, deserted, abandoned, or exposed, is guilty of an offence and liable, on summary conviction, to a fine not exceeding one thousand dollars, or to imprisonment for a period not exceeding one year, or to both fine and imprisonment.

Nova Scotia: Children's Services Act

No specific provision.

New Brunswick: The Child Welfare Act

No specific provision.

Quebec: Youth Protection Act

39. (2) Whosoever wilfully and without valid excuse expose a child to a serious moral or physical danger or, being responsible for such child, neglects to protect him from such danger in a manner and in circumstances not covered by the Criminal Code, is liable, on summary proceeding, to a fine not exceeding three hundred dollars or to imprisonment not exceeding one year, or to both penalties together, in addition to the costs.

If the judge finds the accused guilty of the offence charged against him, he may suspend sentence and impose upon him such order and conditions as he may deem to be in the child's interest; upon proof that such order has not been obeyed or that such conditions have not been fulfilled, the judge shall then pronounce final sentence and order the same to be carried out.

Ontario: The Child Welfare Act

40. (1) Any person having the care, custody, control or charge of a child who abandons, deserts or fails to support the child or inflicts cruelty or ill-treatment

154

upon the child not constituting an assault or otherwise fails to protect the child is guilty of an offence and on summary conviction before a judge is liable to a fine of not more than $500 or to imprisonment for a term of not more than one year, or to both.

Manitoba: The Child Welfare Act

38. (1) Any person having the care, custody, control or charge of a child and who inflicts cruelty or ill-treatment upon the child or fails to protect the child is guilty of an offence punishable on summary conviction.

Saskatchewan: The Family Services Act

76. A person who, having the care, custody, control or charge of a child under the age of sixteen years, abuses, abandons or exposes the child or causes or procures the child to be abused, abandoned or exposed is guilty of an offence and liable on summary conviction to a fine not exceeding $200 and in default of payment to imprisonment for a term not exceeding thirty days.

Alberta: The Child Welfare Act

42. A person who has the care, custody, control or charge of a child and who

    (a) ill-treats, neglects, abandons or harmfully exposes the child, or

    (b) causes or procures the ill-treatment, neglect, abandonment or harmful exposure of the child,

is guilty of an offence and liable upon summary conviction to a fine of not more than one thousand dollars and in default of payment to imprisonment for a term not exceeding two years, or to both fine and imprisonment.

British Columbia: The Protection of Children Act

31. Any person who, having the care, custody, control, or charge of a child under the age of nineteen years, ill-treats, neglects, deserts, or abandons or exposes such child, or causes or procures such child to be ill-treated, neglected, deserted, abandoned, or exposed, is liable, on summary conviction, to a fine not exceeding one hundred dollars, or to imprisonment for a period not exceeding one year, or to both fine and imprisonment.

Northwest Territories: The Child Welfare Ordinance

33. (1) No person shall

    . . .

    (c) having the care, custody, control or charge of a child, ill-treat, neglect, desert, abandon or expose such child or procure the ill-treatment, neglect, desertion, abandonment or exposure of such child.

(2) Any person who violates any provision of this Ordinance is guilty of an offence and liable upon summary conviction to a fine not exceeding five hundred dollars, or to imprisonment for a term not exceeding six months, or to both such fine and imprisonment.

Yukon: The Child Welfare Ordinance

24. No person shall

    . . .

    (c) having the care, control or charge of a child, ill-treat, neglect, desert, abandon or expose such child or procure the ill-treatment, neglect, desertion, abandonment or exposure of such child.

. . .

26. Any person who

    (a)   violates the provision of sections 18, 24 or 25

    . . .

is guilty of an offence and liable upon summary conviction to a fine not exceeding five hundred dollars or to imprisonment for a term not exceeding six months, or to both fine and imprisonment.[4]

1. S. West, "Acute Periosteal Swelling in Several Young Infants of the Same Family," *Brit. Med. J.*, 1888, 1:856.
2. J. S. Stone, "Acute Epiphyseal and Periosteal Infections in Infants and Children," *Boston Med. and Surg.*, 1907, 156:842.
3. J. Caffey, "Multiple Fractures in the Long Bones of Infants Suffering From Chronic Subdural Hematoma," *Am. J. Roentgenol.*, 1946, 56:163.
4. F. D. Ingraham and H. L. Heyl, "Subdural Hematoma in Infancy and Childhood," *J. Am. Med. Assoc.*, 1939, 112:198-204.
5. R. A. Groff and F. C. Grant, "Chronic Subdural Hematoma; Collective Review," *Internat. Abstr. Surg.*, 1942, 74:9-20.
6. C. H. Kempe, F. N. Silverman, B. F. Steele, W. Droegemueller, and H. K. Silver, "The Battered Child Syndrome," *J. Am. Med. Assoc.*, 1962, 181:17.
7. B. Schlesinger, "Battered Children and Damaged Parents," *Canada's Health and Welfare*, 19 (No. 9, November 1964):3.
8. *J. Am. Med. Assoc.*, Editorial, 1962, 181:42.
9. R. Burns, "The Battered Child Syndrome," *Louisiana State Med. Soc.*, 1963, 115:332-334.
10. "The Battered Child," *Newsweek*, Vol. 71, No. 23, June 3, 1968, p. 68.
11. *Child Abuse and Neglect Reports*, National Center on Child Abuse and Neglect, U.S. Dept. of Health, Education, and Welfare, Washington, D.C.: DHEW Publication No. (OHD) 76-30086, June 1976, p. 1.
12. A. C. Fairburn and C. Hunt, "Caffey's Third Syndrome – A Critical Evaluation (The Battered Baby)," *Med. Sci. and the Law*, 1964, 4:123-126.
13. *Child Abuse and Neglect*, Report to the House of Commons by the Standing Committee on Health, Welfare and Social Affairs, Ottawa, July 7, 1976, pp. 35-36.
14. R. E. Helfer and C. H. Kempe, eds., *Child Abuse and Neglect, The Family and the Community*, Cambridge, Mass: Ballinger Publishing Co., 1976, p. xvii.
15. V. J. Fontana, D. Donovan, and R. Wong, "The Maltreatment Syndrome in Children," *The New England J. Med.*, 1963, 269:1389-1394.
16. W. Ziering, "The Battered Baby Syndrome," *J. Ped.*, 1964, 65:321-322.
17. F. V. Harper, "The Physician, the Battered Child, and the Law," *Pediatrics*, 1965, 31:899-902.
18. F. M. Nomura, "The Battered Child Syndrome," *Hawaii Med. J.*, 1966, 25:387-94.
19. "Welfare of Children," Editorial in *Brit. Med. J.*, 1963, 5360:761-762.
20. M. J. Paulson and P. R. Blake, "The Abused and Battered Child: A Review," *Trauma* 9 (No. 4, December 1967):6.

21. C. H. Kempe, "Pediatric Implications of the Battered Child Syndrome," *Archives of Diseases in Childhood*, 1971, 46:31.
22. H. P. Chase and H. P. Martin, "Undernutrition and Child Development," *The New England J. Med.*, 1970, 282:933-939.
23. B. S. Koel, "Failure to Thrive and Fatal Injury as a Continuum," *Amer. J. Dis. Child.*, 118:565-567.
24. J. T. Weston, "The Pathology of Child Abuse," in *The Battered Child*, edited by R. E. Helfer and C. H. Kempe, Chicago and London: University of Chicago Press, 1968, pp. 77-100.
25. R. Gillespie, "The Battered Child Syndrome: Thermal and Caustic Manifestations," *J. of Trauma*, 1965, 5:523-534.
26. M. Van Stolk, "Beaten Women – Battered Children," *Children Today*, Vol. 5, No. 2, March-April 1976, pp. 8-12.
27. R. J. Gelles, "Violence and Pregnancy: A Note on the Extent of the Problem and Needed Services," *The Family Coordinator*, January 1975.
28. *Ibid.*
29. David G. Gil, *Violence against Children*, Cambridge, Mass: Harvard University Press, 1970, p. 116.
30. Cyril Greenland, *Child Abuse in Ontario*, Research Report 3, Ontario Ministry of Community and Social Services, Research and Planning Branch, November 1973, pp. 14, 47.
31. S. Zalba, "Battered Children," *Transaction*, July-August 1971.
32. David G. Gil, "Violence Against Children," *J. of Marriage and the Family*, November 1971.
33. Testimony of Douglas J. Besharov, Director, National Center on Child Abuse and Neglect, before the House of Representatives Committee on Science and Technology (DISPAC Subcommittee), February 14, 1978, pp. 17-18.
34. M. J. Paulson and P. R. Blake, *op. cit.*, p. 71.
35. B. F. Steele and C. B. Pollock, "A Psychiatric Study of Parents Who Abuse Infants and Small Children," in Helfer and Kempe, *The Battered Child*, pp. 106-108.
36. James W. Prescott, "Body Pleasure and the Origins of Violence," *The Futurist*, April 1975.
37. B. F. Steele and C. B. Pollock, *op. cit.*, p. 107.
38. *Ibid.*, p. 106.
39. George F. Solomon, "Psychodynamic Aspects of Aggression, Hostility, and Violence," in *Violence and the Struggle for Existence*, ed. by David N. Daniels, Marshall F. Gilula, Frank M. Ochberg. Boston: Little, Brown and Co., 1970, p. 72. Work of the Committee on Violence of the Department of Psychiatry, Stanford University School of Medicine.
40. *The Select Committee on Violence in Marriage, Minutes of Evidence*, February 26, 1975, House of Commons, London, England.
41. R. J. Gelles, *The Violent Home: A Study of Physical Aggression between Husbands and Wives*, Beverly Hills, Calif., and London: Sage Publications, 1972.
42. Jerry J. I. Cooper, "Discussion of Family Structure, Family

Treatment Programs, and Help for Abusing Parents," in *Child Abuse: Its Treatment and Prevention, An Interdisciplinary Approach*, M. Van Stolk, ed. To be published by McClelland and Stewart, Toronto, 1979.

43. Joseph Mayer and Rebecca Black, "The Relationship between Alcoholism and Child Abuse/Neglect," in *Currents in Alcoholism*, Volume II, ed. by Frank A. Seixas, New York: Greene and Stratton, 1977, pp. 429-444.

44. Val D. MacMurray, "The Effect and Nature of Alcohol Abuse in Cases of Child Neglect (As Reported in the Child Protection Registry of Alberta)." Presented at the 9th World Congress of Sociology, Uppsala, Sweden, August 14-19, 1978.

45. Ann P. Streisguth, "Maternal Alcoholism and the Outcome of Pregnancy: A Review of the Fetal Alcohol Syndrome," in *Alcoholism Problems in Women and Children*, ed. by Milton Greenblatt and Marc A. Schuckit, New York: Grune and Stratton, 1976, pp. 251-274.

46. David Jensen, "Fetal Alcohol Syndrome: Chemical Abuse of Children," *American Humane Magazine*, Vol. 66, No. 2, February 1978, p. 18.

47. Ruth Kempe and C. Henry Kempe, "Assessing Family Pathology," in R. E. Helfer and C. Henry Kempe, eds., *Child Abuse and Neglect, The Family and the Community*, Cambridge, Mass: Ballinger Pub. Co., 1976, p. 118.

48. B. F. Steele and C. B. Pollock, *op. cit.*, p. 108.

49. *Ibid.*, p. 109.

50. Ruth Kempe and C. Henry Kempe, "Assessing Family Pathology," *op. cit.*, p. 117.

51. *Ibid.*, p. 118.

52. B. F. Steele and C. B. Pollock, *op. cit.*, p. 109.

53. David G. Gil, *Violence against Children*, p. 6.

54. Blair Justice and David F. Duncan, "Life Crisis as a Precursor to Child Abuse," *Public Health Reports*, Vol. 91, No. 2, March-April 1976, pp. 110-115.

55. David G. Gil, *Violence against Children*, p. 144.

56. *Ibid.*, pp. 133-148.

57. N. A. Polansky, C. Hally, and N. F. Polansky, *Profile of Neglect. A Survey of the State of Knowledge of Child Neglect*. Washington, D.C.: Community Services Admin., Social and Rehabilitation Services, DHEW, 1975, p. 5.

58. J. M. Giovannoni and R. Becerra, *The Relative Seriousness of Incidents of Child Abuse and Neglect*. Report to Social and Rehabilitation Service, Offs. of Research and Demonstration, DHEW, 1977.

NOTES TO CHAPTER 2

1. D. G. Gil, "Incidence of Child Abuse and Demographic Characteristics of Persons Involved," in *The Battered Child*, ed. R. E.

Helfer and C. H. Kempe, Chicago and London: The University of Chicago Press, 1968, pp. 24-25.

2. L. Young, *Wednesday's Children*, New York: McGraw-Hill, 1964.

3. B. F. Steele in "Proceedings of Conference on Patterns of Parental Behaviour Leading to Physical Abuse of Children," unpublished (University of Colorado, School of Medicine, 1966), quoted in D. G. Gil's *Violence Against Children*, p. 31.

4. B. F. Steele and C. B. Pollock, "A Psychiatric Study of Parents Who Abuse Infants and Small Children," in Helfer and Kempe, *The Battered Child*, p. 120.

5. C. B. Pollock in an address given to the Alberta Human Rights Association, Edmonton, Alberta, 1971.

6. B. F. Steele, "Violence in Our Society," *The Pharos of Alpha Omega Alpha*, 1970, 33:44.

7. B. F. Steele and C. B. Pollock, "A Psychiatric Study of Parents Who Abuse Infants and Small Children," in Helfer and Kempe, *The Battered Child*, p. 110.

8. B. F. Steele, "Violence in Our Society," p. 44.

9. B. F. Steele and C. B. Pollock, "A Psychiatric Study of Parents Who Abuse Infants and Small Children," p. 131.

10. *Ibid.*, p. 110.

11. B. F. Steele, "Violence in Our Society," p. 44.

12. W. Eckhardt and N. Z. Alcock, "Ideology and Personality in War/Peace Attitudes," *J. of Soc. Psychology*, 1970, 81:105-116.

13. J. Henry, *Culture Against Man*, New York: Random House, 1964.

14. H. Arendt, *On Violence*, New York: Harcourt, Brace and World, 1970.

15. C. Bay, *The Structure of Freedom*, New York: Atheneum, 1965.

16. G. Leonard, *Education and Ecstasy*, New York: Delta Books, 1968.

17. C. Hampden-Turner, *Radical Man, The Process of Psychosocial Development*, Cambridge, Mass.: Schenkman Publishing Co., 1970.

18. H. Sherriff, "The Abused Child," *J.S.C.M.A.*, 1964, 60:191-193.

19. J. T. Corbett, "Psychiatrist Reviews the Battered Child Syndrome and Mandatory Reporting Legislation," *North-West Medical* (No. 63, December 1964): 920-922.

20. G. C. Curtis, "Violence Breeds Violence – Perhaps," *American J. Psychiat.*, 1963, 120:386.

21. M. J. Paulson and P. R. Blake, "The Abused, Battered and Maltreated Child: A Review," *Trauma* 9 (No. 4, December 1967): 56-57.

22. B. F. Steele and C. B. Pollock, *op. cit.*, p. 111.

23. S. R. Zalba, "The Abused Child II: A Typology for Classification and Treatment," *Social Work* 12 (No. 1, January 1967): 70-79.

24. B. F. Steele and C. B. Pollock, *op. cit.*, p. 129.

25. *Ibid.*

26. C. B. Pollock, "Early Case Findings as a Means of Prevention of Child Abuse," in *The Battered Child*, p. 151.
27. *Ibid.*, p. 152.
28. B. F. Steele and C. B. Pollock, "A Psychiatric Study of Parents Who Abuse Infants and Small Children," in *The Battered Child*, p. 109.
29. E. Davoren, "The Role of the Social Worker," in *The Battered Child*, pp. 232-235.
30. J. T. Weston, "Summary of Neglect and Traumatic Cases," in *The Battered Child*, pp. 232-235.
31. *Ibid.*, p. 155.
32. E. Davoren, "The Role of the Social Worker," in *The Battered Child*, p. 156.
33. B. Steele, "Proceedings of Conference on Patterns of Parental Behaviour Leading to Physical Abuse of Children," *op. cit.*, pp. 31-33.
34. James W. Prescott, "Body Pleasure and the Origins of Violence," *The Futurist*, April 1975.

NOTES TO CHAPTER 3

1. D. G. Gil, *Violence against Children*, p. 122.
2. *Ibid.*, p. 128.
3. L. Young, *Wednesday's Children: A Study of Child Neglect and Abuse*, New York: McGraw-Hill, 1964, pp. 49-54.
4. J. Rubin, "The Need for Intervention-Preventing Maltreatment of Children," *Public Welfare*, 1966, 24:230-235.
5. B. F. Steele and C. B. Pollock, *op. cit.*, p. 104.
6. D. G. Gil, *Violence against Children*, p. 141.
7. B. F. Steele and C. B. Pollock, *op. cit.*, p. 128.
8. B. Berelson and G. A. Steiner, *Human Behaviour: An Inventory of Scientific Findings*, New York: Harcourt, Brace and World Inc., 1964, pp. 73-84.
9. David G. Gil, *Violence against Children*, pp. 7-12.
10. W. H. Ferry, "Masscomm as Guru," *Mass Communications*, Santa Barbara: The Center for the Study of Democratic Institutions, 1966, p. 14.
11. David G. Gil, *Violence against Children*, pp. 142-143.

NOTES TO CHAPTER 4

1. David G. Gil, *Violence against Children*, p. 55.
2. R. Benedict, *Patterns of Culture*, New York: Mentor Books, 1957, p. 93.
3. G. Gorer, "Man Has No 'Killer' Instinct," in *Man and Aggression*, edited by Ashley Montagu, London, Oxford, New York: Oxford University Press, 1968, p. 34.

4. M. Mead, *Coming of Age in Samoa*, New York: Morrow, 1928.
5. B. Malinowski, *Sex and Repression in Savage Society*, New York: Harcourt, Brace and World, Inc., 1927.
6. James W. Prescott, "Body Pleasure and the Origins of Violence; *The Futurist*, April 1975.
7. S. R. Zalba, "Battered Children," *Trans-Action*, 1971, 9/10:61.
8. J. H. Pollack, "What You Can Do to Help Stop Violence, An Interview with Dr. John P. Spiegel, Director, Lemberg Centre for the Study of Violence," Brandeis University, in *Family Circle* 73 (No. 4, October 1968):78.
9. S. R. Zalba, "The Abused Child II: A Typology for Classification and Treatment," *Social Work* 12 (No. 1, January 1967): 70-79.
10. B. F. Steele, C. B. Pollock and E. Davoren, "Observations on the Treatment of Parents Who Attack Their Children." Project on the Battered Child Syndrome, conducted jointly by the Dept. of Psychiatry and Dept. of Pediatrics, University of Colorado Medical Centre. Unpublished. 1966.
11. R. Galdston, "Observations on Children Who Have Been Physically Abused and Their Parents," *Am. Psychiatric Assoc.*, 122 (No. 4, May 1965):440-443.
12. F. A. Allen, "Maltreatment Syndrome in Children," *Canadian Nurse*, 1966, 62:40-42.
13. J. D. Delsordo, "Protective Casework for Abused Children," *Children* 10 (No. 6, December 1963):213-218.
14. B. F. Steele and C. B. Pollock, "A Psychiatric Study of Parents Who Abuse Infants and Small Children," in Helfer and Kempe, *The Battered Child*, p. 110.
15. R. Galdston, *op. cit.*, pp. 440-443.
16. S. K. Steinmetz and M. A. Straus, "The Family as Cradle of Violence," *Society*, September-October 1973, 10(6), pp. 50-56.
17. Dial Torgerson, "In Some Places Children Do Grow Up Too Fast," *The Spectator*, January 11, 1973 (*The Los Angeles Times*).
18. *Ibid.*
19. Joe Jacobs, ed., *Child Abuse, Neglect, Deprivation and the Family Syndrome*, Sherbrooke, Quebec: The Mental Health Committee of the Canadian Paediatric Society, April 1976, p. 3.

NOTES TO CHAPTER 5

1. R. Galdston, "Observations on Children Who Have Been Physically Abused and Their Parents," *Am. Psychiatric Assoc.*, 122 (No. 4, May 1965):440-443.
2. K. S. Bernhardt, *Discipline and Child Guidance*, New York: McGraw-Hill, 1964, pp. 63-70.
3. L. Silver, W. Baxton and C. Dublin, "Child Abuse Laws – Are They Enough?," *J.A.M.A.*, 1967, 199:65.
4. R. G. Atkinson, M. N. Clark, M. G. Lukas and G. S. W. Wickett, "The Battered Child Syndrome." Unpublished thesis

for Master's Degree Social Work, University of British Columbia, 1965, p. 47.

5. H. E. Boardman, "A Project to Rescue Children from Inflicted Injuries," *Social Work 7* (No. 1, January 1962):48.

6. W. Ziering, "The Battered Baby Syndrome," *J. of Ped.*, 1964, 65:321-322.

7. V. J. Fontana, "Recognition of Maltreatment and Prevention of Battered Child Syndrome," *Pediatrics*, 1966, 38:1078.

8. H. Kearns, "Battered Baby Syndrome, Concerned People Mobilize Against 'Shocking Injustice'," *Montreal Star*, July 18, 1970, p. 53.

9. J. T. Weston, "Summary of Neglect and Traumatic Cases," in Helfer and Kempe, *The Battered Child*, pp. 232-235.

10. H. Jacobziner, "Rescuing the Battered Child," *American J. of Nursing*, 64 (No. 6, June 1964):97.

11. R. G. Atkinson *et al., op. cit.*, p. 39.

12. S. R. Zalba, "Battered Children," *Trans-Action*, 1971, 9/10:61.

13. R. E. Helfer, "The Responsibility and Role of the Physician," in Helfer and Kempe. *The Battered Child*, 2nd edition, 1974, p. 33.

14. G. H. Earl, "Ten Thousand Children Battered and Starved," *Today's Health*, September, 1965, p. 51.

15. S. H. Fisher, "Skeletal Manifestations of Parent-Induced Trauma in Infants and Children," *Southern Medical Journal*, 1958, 51:956-960.

16. R. Galdston, "Observations on Children Who Have Been Physically Abused and Their Parents," pp. 440-443.

17. V. J. Fontana, "Recognition for Maltreatment and Prevention of the Battered Child Syndrome," *Pediatrics*, 1966, 38:1078.

18. M. J. Paulson and P. R. Blake, "The Abused, Battered and Maltreated Child: A Review," *Trauma* 9 (No. 4, December 1967), p. 105.

19. J. Roberts, "Characteristics of the Abused Child and His Family: An Agency Study." Unpublished thesis submitted for course in Social Work, Carleton University School of Social Work, 1968, p. 78.

20. *Ibid.*, pp. 114-115.

21. R. E. Helfer, "The Responsibility and Role of the Physician," in Helfer and Kempe, *The Battered Child*, pp. 43-57.

22. S. R. Zalba, "Battered Children," *Trans-Action*, *op. cit.*, p. 60.

23. R. E. Helfer, "The Responsibility and Role of the Physician," *op. cit.*, p. 47.

24. J. T. Weston, "A Summary of Neglect and Traumatic Cases," in Helfer and Kempe, *The Battered Child*, pp. 232-233.

25. H. B. Cotnam, "The Battered Child Syndrome or The Maltreatment Syndrome in Children," *Canadian Assoc. of Medical Students and Interns Journal*, 24 (No. 3, October 1965), p. 12.

NOTES TO CHAPTER 6

1. The material for this chapter is based on confidential interviews

with adults who were battered in their childhood. This material has been gathered over the past fourteen years and was initially begun as part of the research for *Man and Woman*, by M. Van Stolk, Toronto: McClelland and Stewart, 1968.

2. R. D. Laing, *The Divided Self*, Harmondsworth: Penguin Books, 1965, pp. 39-65.

3. Marshall H. Klaus and John H. Kennell, *Maternal-Infant Bonding*, Saint Louis: The C.V. Mosby Co., 1976.

4. John Bowlby, *Attachment and Loss, Vol. 1*, New York: Basic Books, Inc., 1969.

5. H. F. Harlow, "Love in Infant Monkeys," in *The Nature and Nurture of Behavior*. Readings from *Scientific American*, San Francisco: W. H. Freeman and Co., 1973, p. 94.

6. S. Rado, "The Psychical Effects of Intoxication," *Psychoanalytic Review*, Vol. 18, 1931, pp. 69-84.

7. B. F. Steele and C. B. Pollock, "A Psychiatric Study of Parents Who Abuse Infants and Small Children," in Helfer and Kempe, *The Battered Child*, p. 115.

8. B. Malinowski, *Sex and Repression in Savage Society*, New York: Harcourt, Brace and World, 1927.

9. Henry K. Silver and Marcia Finkelstein, "Deprivation Dwarfism," *The J. of Pediatrics*, Vol. 70, No. 3, Part 1, pp. 317-324, March 1967.

10. Karl Evang, Director-General of Health Services of Norway, in a 1973 report to the World Health Organization.

11. *Child Abuse and Neglect*, Report to the House of Commons by the Standing Committee on Health, Welfare and Social Affairs, Ottawa, July 1976, pp. 55-56.

12. Roger W. McIntire, "Parenthood Training or Mandatory Birth Control: Take Your Choice," *Psychology Today*, October 1973.

13. *Mental Health Statistics*, Statistics Canada, Vol. I, 1972.

14. *Ibid.*

15. *Ibid.*

16. *Ibid.*

17. *Mental Health Statistics*, Statistics Canada, Vol. III, 1973.

18. *Ibid.*

19. Study: *Adaptive Planning – Mental Illness, Some of the Costs* (Mental Health/Canada), June 1975.

20. *One Million Children* – (Mental Health/Canada Report) 1970.

21. *Mental Health Statistics*, Statistics Canada, Vol. I, 1972.

22. *Expectancy of Admissions to Canadian Psychiatric Institutions*, Dominion Bureau of Statistics, 1968.

23. The Canadian Mental Health Association, January 29, 1976.

NOTES TO CHAPTER 7

1. Dr. C. B. Pollock in an address presented to the Alberta Human Rights Association, Edmonton, Alberta, 1971.

2. R. E. Helfer, "The Responsibility and Role of the Physician," in Helfer and Kempe, *The Battered Child*, p. 45.

3. *Ibid.*, p. 48.

4. E. Elmer, "Identification of Abused Children," *Children* 10 (No. 5, September-October 1963):180-184.

5. J. L. Gwinn, *et. al.*, "Radiological Case of the Month," *Amer. J. Dis. Child.*, 1965, 109:457-458.

6. R. E. Helfer, "The Responsibility and Role of the Physician," in Helfer and Kempe, *The Battered Child*, p. 46.

7. Jerry J. I. Cooper, "Discussion of Family Structure, Family Treatment Programs and Help for Abusing Parents," in M. Van Stolk, ed., *Child Abuse: Its Treatment and Prevention, An Interdisciplinary Approach*. To be published by McClelland and Stewart, Toronto, 1979.

8. Sydney Segal, "Child Abuse: Hospital Programs," *ibid.*

9. A. N. Guthkelch, "Infantile Subdural Hematoma and Its Relationship to Whiplash Injuries," *Brit. Med. J.*, 1971, 2:430-431.

10. "Infant Victims of 'Whiplash'," *Science Digest*, June 1968, pp. 68-69.

11. John Caffey, "On the Theory and Practice of Shaking Infants. Its Potential Residual Effects of Permanent Brain Damage and Mental Retardation," *Amer. J. Dis. Child.*, Vol. 124, No. 2, August 1972, pp. 161-169.

12. *Ibid.*

13. R. E. Helfer, "The Responsibility and Role of the Physician," in Helfer and Kempe, *The Battered Child*, p. 46.

14. Robert Bates, "Child Abuse and Neglect: A Medical Priority," in Van Stolk, ed.

15. H. B. Cotnam, "The Battered Child Syndrome (Child Abuse and Neglect)," *ibid.*

16. Sydney Segal, "Child Abuse: Hospital Programs," *ibid.*

17. Robert J. Ford, Brain S. Smistek, and James T. Glass, "Photography of Suspected Child Abuse and Maltreatment," *Biomedical Communications*, Vol. 3, No. 4, July 1975, p. 12.

18. *Ibid.*, pp. 12-16.

19. R. E. Helfer, "The Responsibility and Role of the Physician," in Helfer and Kempe, *The Battered Child*, 2nd edition, 1974, p. 33.

20. J. T. Corbett, "A Psychiatrist Reviews the Battered Child Syndrome and Mandatory Reporting Legislation," *Northwest Medicine*, 63:920-922, 1962.

21. Eleanor LeBourdais, "Look Again," *Canadian Hospital*, Vol. 49, No. 1, January 1972.

22. C. Greenland and E. Rosenblatt, *The Home Accidents and Injuries Study* (HAIS), Ontario Ministry of Community and Social Services, 1974.

23. L. B. Silver, et al., "Child Abuse Laws: Are They Enough?", *J.A.M.A.*, 199:101-104, 1967.

24. *Child Abuse and Neglect*, Report to the House of Commons by the Standing Committee on Health, Welfare, and Social Affairs, Ottawa, July 1976, p. 44.

25. R. E. Helfer, "The Responsibility and Role of the Physician," in Helfer and Kempe, *The Battered Child*, 2nd edition, 1974, p. 33.
26. David M. Steinberg, "The Child Welfare Act, Part II, Children in Need of Protection," in *Family Law in the Family Courts*, H.T.G. Andrews, ed. Toronto: Carswell Ltd., 1973, p. 76.
27. See Section 4 (2) of the *Canada Evidence Act*, R.S.C. 1970, c. E-10.
28. There may be advantages in making the spouse compellable rather than just competent, since having to exercise choice might expose the spouse to prior pressure and subsequent recrimination.
29. In the proposed U.S. Federal Rules of Evidence, Rule 505(a) provides that "An accused in a criminal proceeding has a privilege to prevent his spouse from testifying against him," but sub-rule (c) provides that "There is no privilege under this rule in proceedings in which one spouse is charged with a crime against the person or property of the other or of a child of either."
30. Law Reform Commission of Canada, Evidence Study Paper No. 1, at 4-5.
31. *Medical Act*, S.Q. 1973, c. 46, s. 40; Art. 308 of the *Quebec Code of Civil Procedure*, as amended by 1975, c. 6, s. 96; *Descarreaux v. Jacques*, [1969] B. R. 1109 (Quebec C.A.).
32. Margaret Hughes, "The Law as It Affects the Physician in Canada in Child Abuse Cases," in Van Stolk, ed., forthcoming.
33. Monrad G. Paulsen, "The Law and Abused Children," in Helfer and Kempe, *The Battered Child*, pp. 195-199.
34. *Ibid.*, p. 195.
35. J. W. Polier and K. McDonald, "The Family Court in an Urban Setting," in R. E. Helfer and C. H. Kempe, eds., *Helping the Battered Child and His Family*, Philadelphia and Toronto: J. B. Lippincott Co., 1972.
36. Committee on Infant and Pre-School Child, American Academy of Pediatrics, "Maltreatment of Children, the Physically Abused Child" (1966), 37 *Pediatrics*, pp. 377-380.
37. *The Child Welfare Act*, R.S.A. 1970, c. 45, s. 41 as amended by S. A. 1973, c. 15, s. 8.
38. *Protection of Children Act*, R.S.B.C. 1960, c. 303, s. 7(2) as amended by S.B.C. 1974, c. 69, s. 1.
39. *The Child Welfare Act*, S.M. 1974, c. 30, s. 36.
40. *The Child Welfare Act*, S. Nfld. 1972, No. 37, s. 49.
41. *Children's Services Act*, S.N.S. 1976, c. 8, ss. 72, 82.
42. *The Child Welfare Act*, R.S.O. 1970, c. 64, s. 41.
43. *Youth Protection Act*, R.S.Q. 1964, c. 220, as amended by S.Q. 1974, c. 59, ss. 14j, 14k.
44. *The Family Services Act 1973*, S.S. 1973, c. 38, s. 16.
45. *Child Welfare Ordinance*, R.O.Y.T. 1971, c. C-4, ss. 25, 26.
46. Margaret Hughes, *op. cit.*
47. *Robison v. Wical et al.*, San Luis Obispo Superior Court, No. 37607 (settled Oct. 24. 1972).

48. Society of Hospital Attorneys, 6 *American Hosp. Assn. Newsletter* 5 (1973).

NOTES TO CHAPTER 8

1. Plato, *De Republica*, I, 309.
2. Plato, *De Legibus*, VI, 376.
3. Aristotle, *Politics*, I, ii, 7; *Nichomachean Ethics*, VIII, 10.
4. Exodus, 21, *The New English Bible*, Oxford: Oxford Univ. Press, 1970.
5. Colonial Laws of Massachusetts with Supplements, 1672-1686.
6. Mason P. Thomas, Jr., "Child Abuse and Neglect: Part I. Historical Overview, Legal Matrix and Social Perspectives" (1972), 50 *N. Carolina Law Review* 293, note 44 at 305.
7. Gail Garinger, "Protecting Children: Innovations in Policy and Procedures" (Spring 1977), 28 *Harvard Law School Bulletin*, p. 29.
8. David J. Rothman, *The Discovery of the Asylum: Social Order and Disorder in the New Republic*, Boston: Little Brown, 1971, p. 29.
9. Proverbs, 23:13-14.
10. David G. Gil, *Violence against Children – Physical Child Abuse in the United States*, Cambridge, Mass.: Harvard University Press, 1970.
11. Simon Kreindler, "Psychiatric Treatment for the Abusing Parent and the Abused Child," *Canadian Psychiatric Assoc. J.*, Vol. 21, No. 5, 1976, p. 278.
12. Richard Gelles, University of Rhode Island, in a presentation to the Annual Meeting of the American Association for the Advancement of Science, Denver, Colorado, February 25, 1977.
13. *Newsweek*, October 10, 1977, p. 112.
14. M. Rood-de-Boer, State University, Utrecht, and Catholic University, Tilburg, in her paper "Children's Suicide." A Report Presented to the interdisciplinary Second World Conference of The International Society on Family Law dealing with Violence in the Family, Montreal, June 13-17, 1977.
15. Eddy Polak, Professional Development Animator, Quebec Association for Children with Learning Disabilities, in his presentation to the Senate Subcommittee on Childhood Experiences as Causes of Criminal Behaviour, May 31, 1977. In *Minutes of Proceedings of the Subcommittee on Childhood Experiences as Causes of Criminal Behaviour*, May 31, 1977, Ottawa, Appendix "I-C," p. 104.
16. *Premier Rapport d'Activité*, Comité pour la protection de la jeunesse, Ministère de la Justice, Gouvernement du Québec, Editeur officiel du Québec, 1977.
17. *Help for Abused Children*, brochure prepared by Comité pour la protection de la jeunesse, Montreal, 1975.

18. *The Abused Child*, Alberta Health and Social Development, 1974.
19. *Ibid.*
20. *Ibid.*
21. *Children's Services Act*, S.N.S. 1976, c. 8, s. 42.
22. *Child Welfare Ordinance*, R.O.Y.T. 1971, c. C-4, s. 25 creates the obligation. Enforcement is via section 26.
23. British Columbia: *Protection of Children Act*, R.S.B.C. 1960, c. 303, s. 7(2), as amended by 1967, c. 38 and 1974, c. 69 creates the obligation. Enforcement via *Summary Convictions Act*, R.S.B.C. 1960, c. 373, s. 5, as amended by 1969, c. 35 and 1972, c. 60.

    Manitoba: *The Child Welfare Act*, S.M. 1974, c. 30, s. 36 creates the obligation. Enforcement via *The Summary Convictions Act*, R.S.M. 1970, c. S230, s. 4.

    Newfoundland: *The Child Welfare Act*, S. Nfld. 1972, No. 37, s. 49, as amended by 1974, No. 100 creates the obligation. Section 55(2) is the penalty clause.

    Nova Scotia: *Children's Services Act*, S.N.S. 1976, c. 8, s. 77 creates the obligation. Penalty clause is section 82.

    Quebec: *Youth Protection Act*, R.S.Q. 1964, c. 220, s. 14j, as amended by 1974, c. 59 creates the obligation. Enforcement via *Summary Proceedings Act*, R.S.Q. 1964, c. 35, s. 66, as amended by 1970, c. 11.

    Saskatchewan: *The Family Services Act*, S.S. 1973, c. 38, s. 16(1) creates the obligation. Enforcement is via *The Summary Offences Procedure Act*, 1969, c. 62, s. 2A(1), as amended by 1970, c. 70 and via the *Criminal Code*, R.S.C. 1970, c. C-34, s. 722(1).
24. *Child Welfare Act*, R.S.N.B. 1973, c. C-4, s. 30.
25. *The Child Welfare Act*, R.S.O. 1970, c. 64, s. 41.
26. H. A. Allard, "Family Courts in Canada," in *Studies in Canadian Family Law*, D. Mendes da Costa, ed., Toronto: Butterworth's, 1972, p. 6.
27. *Ibid.*
28. *Ibid.*, p. 7.
29. D. K. Skoler and C. W. Tenney, Jr., "Attorney Representation in Juvenile Court" (1964), 4 *J. Family Law* 77; reprinted in *Children in the Courts*, G.G. Newman, ed., Ann Arbor: Institute of Continuing Legal Education, 1967, p. 187.
30. M. Van Stolk, *The Battered Child in Canada*, Toronto: McClelland and Stewart, 1972, p. 77.
31. F. M. Fraser, "Children in Need of Protection," in *Studies in Canadian Family Law*, pp. 83-85.

32. Dr. Karl Evang, Director-General of Health Services of Norway, in a 1973 report to the World Health Organization; Henry K. Silver and Marcia Finkelstein, "Deprivation Dwarfism" (1967), 3 *The Journal of Pediatrics* 70, pp. 317-324.

33. T. T. Becker, "Protecting Legal Rights through Judicial Process," in *Second National Symposium on Child Abuse*, Denver, Colorado: The American Humane Assoc., Children's Division, 1973, p. 48.

34. M. Van Stolk, *The Battered Child in Canada*, p. 76.

35. *In re S.* (1965), 46 Misc. 2d 161, 259 N.Y.S. 2d 164 (N.Y. Fam. Ct.); *Re A.M.* (1968), 22 R.F.L. 78 (Alta. Fam. Ct.).

36. M. Van Stolk, p. 76.

37. F. M. Fraser, p. 79.

38. *Criminal Code*, supra fn. 10, section 168(1).

39. *Ibid.*, s. 197(1).

40. *Ibid.*, s. 200.

41. *Ibid.*, s. 204.

42. *Ibid.*, s. 205(1).

43. *Ibid.*, ss. 212, 217 and 216.

44. *Ibid.*, s. 229.

45. Joseph A. Poss, "Urban Police," in Van Stolk, ed.

46. Vincent De Francis, *Protecting the Child Victim of Sex Crimes Committed by Adults, Final Report*, Denver, Colorado: The American Humane Association, Children's Division, 1969, p. vii, p. 56.

47. Judianne Densen-Gerber and Jean Benward, "Incest as a Causative Factor in Anti-Social Behavior: An Exploratory Study. The Unspeakable Sin of the Father which Must Rest upon the Child." Paper presented at the American Academy of Forensic Sciences 27th Annual Meeting, Chicago, Illinois, February 19, 1975.

48. M. Van Stolk, "The Sexually Abused Child." A Paper presented to the interdisciplinary Second World Conference of The International Society on Family Law dealing with Violence in the Family, Montreal, June 13-17, 1977.

49. Allan Berman and Andrew Siegal, "A Neuropsychological Approach to the Etiology, Prevention, and Treatment of Juvenile Delinquency," in *Child Personality and Psychopathology: Current Topics*, Vol. 3, ed. by Anthony Davids, New York: John Wiley and Sons, 1976, p. 264.

50. The Fifth Report of the (B.C.) Royal Commission on Family and Children's Law, *Children and the Law, Part III, Children's Rights*, Vancouver, B.C., March 1975, p. 2.

NOTES TO CHAPTER 9

1. J. Roberts, "Characteristics of the Abused Child and His Family: An Agency Study." Unpublished thesis submitted for course

in social work, Carleton University, School of Social Work, 1968, p. 82.

2. H. Boardman, "A Project to Rescue Children From Inflicted Injuries," *Social Work*, 1962, 7, p. 44.
3. R. E. Helfer, "The Responsibility and Role of the Physician," in *The Battered Child*, pp. 43-57.
4. C. H. Kempe, "Some Problems Encountered by Welfare Departments in the Management of the Battered Child Syndrome," in *The Battered Child*, p. 170.
5. *Ibid.*
6. Norman and Nancy Polansky, "The Current Status on Child Abuse and Child Neglect in This Country." Report to the Joint Commission on Mental Health for Children (February, 1968), quoted in D. G. Gil, *Violence Against Children*, pp. 44-45.
7. C. H. Kempe, "Some Problems Encountered by Welfare Departments in the Management of the Battered Child Syndrome," in *The Battered Child*, p. 171.
8. J. Roberts, *op. cit.*, p. 95.
9. E. Davoren, "The Role of the Social Worker," in Helfer and Kempe, *The Battered Child*, p. 157.
10. J. Roberts, *op. cit.*, p. 99.
11. J. D. Delsordo, "Protective Casework for Abused Children," *Children* 10 (No. 6, November-December 1963), p. 216.
12. J. Roberts, *op. cit.*, p. 34.
13. Personal correspondence with schools of social work throughout Canada.
14. J. V. Belknap, "Address on Child Abuse," March 9th, 1973, p. 4.
15. *Ibid.*
16. J. Roberts, *op. cit.*, p. 97.
17. Confidential interview with an Alberta social worker.
18. *Child Abuse and Neglect*, Report to the House of Commons by the Standing Committee on Health, Welfare and Social Affairs, Ottawa, July 1976, p. 53.
19. Yude M. Henteleff, "Young Persons in Conflict with the Law." Brief presented to the Solicitor General of Canada on the proposed federal Act, "Young Persons in Conflict With the Law," 1976, p. 3.
20. C. Henry Kempe, "A Vindication of the Rights of Children," 1975 Armstrong Lecture, Denver, Colorado, p. 14.

NOTES TO CHAPTER 10

1. David G. Gil, "What Schools Can Do about Child Abuse", *American Education*, April 1969.
2. Richard J. Gelles, *The Violent Home: A Study of Physical Aggression between Husbands and Wives*, Beverly Hills, Calif. and London: Sage Publications, 1972.
3. Martha Mulligan, "Factors Associated with Violence in the

Family," unpublished master's thesis, Dept. of Sociology, University of Rhode Island, 1977.

4. *Time*, July 11, 1977, p. 12.
5. L. N. Robins, *Deviant Children Grown Up*, Baltimore, Md.: Williams and Wilkins, 1966.
6. William E. Homan, *Child Sense*, Toronto: Bantam, 1970, Chapter 1.
7. Cyril Greenland, *Child Abuse in Ontario*, Research Report 3, Ontario Ministry of Community and Social Services, Queen's Printer, November 1973, p. 2.
8. Robert Bates, "Battered Children and Parents Both in Cycle of Abuse," *Medical Post*, February 18, 1975, p. 44.
9. C. H. Kempe and R. E. Helfer, *Helping the Battered Child and His Family*, Philadelphia: Lippincott, 1972.
10. *The Abused and Battered Child, A Report*, Federation of Women Teachers' Associations of Ontario, August 1976, pp. 10-11.
11. Shirley Amiel, "Child Abuse in Schools," *Northwest Medicine*, 71:808, November 1972.
12. "A Conversation with Abraham H. Maslow," *Psychology Today*, July 1968.
13. John M. Branan, "Negative Human Interaction," *J. of Counselling Psychology*, January, 1972, Vol. 19, No. 1, pp. 81-82.
14. "The Talk of the Town," *The New Yorker*, May 30, 1977.
15. Marge Csapo and Bernie Aag, *Operation Step-Up*, 1974. Report available from the Vancouver Association for Children with Learning Disabilities.

NOTES TO CHAPTER 11

1. *The Gazette*, Montreal, July 30, 1977.
2. *Child Abuse and Neglect*, Report to the House of Commons by the Standing Committee on Health, Welfare and Social Affairs, Ottawa, July 1976, pp. 39-40.
3. *Monthly Vital Statistics Report*, U.S. National Center for Health Statistics, Vol. 25, No. 10, Supplement, December 30, 1976.
4. *Ibid.*, Vol. 24, No. 11, Supplement, February 13, 1976.
5. C. H. Kempe, "Pediatric Implications of the Battered Child Syndrome," in Helfer and Kempe, *The Battered Child*, p. 35.
6. J. Roberts, *Characteristics of the Abused Child and His Family: An Agency Study*, p. 50.
7. J. T. Weston, "A Summary of Neglect and Traumatic Cases," in Helfer and Kempe, *The Battered Child*, pp. 232-235.
8. D. G. Gil, *Violence against Children*, p. 108.
9. From conversation with R. E. Helfer, Department of Human Development, Michigan State University, East Lansing, Michigan.
10. *Child Abuse and Neglect*, Report to the House of Commons by the Standing Committee on Health, Welfare and Social Affairs, Ottawa, July 1976, pp. 19-20.

1. *Child Abuse and Neglect*, Report to the House of Commons by the Standing Committee on Health, Welfare and Social Affairs, Ottawa, July 7, 1976, pp. 51-52.
2. Cumming, Cumming and Edel, "Policeman as Philosopher, Guide and Friend," 12 *Social Problems* 276, 280 (1965).
3. President's Commission on Law Enforcement and Administration of Justice, 92. See also Bullock, "Urban Homicide in Theory and Fact," 45 *Journal of Criminal Law, Criminology and Police Science*, 565, 574 (1955).
4. Raymond I. Parnas, "The Police Response to the Domestic Disturbance," *Wisconsin Law Review*, 1:914-960, 1967.
5. Raymond I. Parnas, "The Relevance of Criminal Law to Interspousal Violence," a Paper Presented to the interdisciplinary Second World Conference of The International Society on Family Law dealing with Violence in the Family, Montreal, June 13-17, 1977.
6. California Rules of Court, New Sentencing Rules for the Superior Court. Effective July 1, 1977.
7. Alvar Nelson, University of Uppsala, Sweden, in his paper "Legal Responses to Child Abuse," A Report Presented to the interdisciplinary Second World Conference of The International Society on Family Law dealing with Violence in the Family, Montreal, June 13-17, 1977.
8. Robert Holmes, "The Police Role in Child Abuse," in *Child Abuse: Its Treatment and Prevention: An Interdisciplinary Approach*, M. Van Stolk, ed. To be published by McClelland and Stewart Ltd., Toronto, 1979.
9. T. T. Becker, "Due Process and Child Protective Proceedings: State Intervention in Family Relations on Behalf of Neglected Children" (1971), 2 *Cumberland-Samford Law Review* 247, p. 16.
10. J. L. Isaacs, "The Role of the Lawyer in Representing Minors in the New Family Court" (1963), 12 *Buffalo Law Review*, 501.
11. *Kent v. The United States* (1966), 383 U.S. 541 at 561, 86 S. Ct. 1045, 16 L.E. 2d 84 per Fortas, J.
12. T. T. Becker, "Protecting Legal Rights through Judicial Process," in *Second National Symposium on Child Abuse*, Denver, Colorado: The American Humane Assoc., Children's Division, 1973, p. 48.
13. F. M. Fraser, "Children in Need of Protection," in *Studies in Canadian Family Law*, Mendes da Costa, ed., Toronto: Butterworth's, 1972, p. 88.
14. *Ibid.*, p. 87.
15. J. L. Isaacs, *op. cit.*
16. Ontario Law Reform Commission, Family Law Project, Study Vol. 10, 1969, p. 249. The Commission's *Report on Family Law*, Part III, Children (1973) endorsed the Study's recommendation; see p. 82 and ch. 5.

17. *Re Helmes* (1976), 13 O.R. (2d) 4 (Ont. H.C.).
18. *Criminal Code*, supra fn. 10, section 43.
19. *Ibid.*, s. 26.
20. Alvar Nelson, *op. cit.*
21. *Ibid.*
22. Judge Victor J. Baum, in his closing presentation to the interdisciplinary Second World Conference of The International Society on Family Law, Montreal, 1977.
23. *Newsweek*, October 10, 1977, p. 112.

NOTES TO CHAPTER 13

1. D. G. Gil, *Violence against Children*, pp. 1-17.
2. A. S. Neill, *Summerhill: A Radical Approach to Child Rearing*, New York: Hart, 1960.
3. A. S. Neill, *Freedom – Not License*, New York: Hart, 1966.
4. B. Bettelheim, *Children of the Dream*, London: Collier-Mac-Millan Co., 1969.
5. W. Eckhardt, "War in the Minds of Men," *War/Peace Report*, 9 (5), 1969, p. 17.
6. A. H. Maslow, *Toward a Psychology of Being*, Princeton: Van Nostrand, 1962.
7. M. V. Van Stolk, *Man and Woman*, Toronto: McClelland and Stewart, 1968, pp. 77-87.
8. G. B. Leonard, *Education and Ecstasy*, New York: Dell Publishing Co., 1968.
9. C. Hampden-Turner, *Radical Man, The Process of Psycho-Social Development*, Cambridge, Mass.: Schenkman Publishing Co., 1970.
10. Children's Division, American Humane Association, *Protecting the Battered Child*, Denver, 1962, p. 18.
11. G. C. Curtis, "Violence Breeds Violence – Perhaps," *Amer. J. of Psychiatry*, 120 (No. 4, October 1963): 386-387.
12. W. M. Easson and R. N. Steinhilber, "Murderous Aggression by Children and Adolescents," *Amer. Med. Assoc. Archives of General Psychiatry* (No. 4, January 1961):27.
13. J. Henry, *Culture Against Man*, New York: Random House, 1964, pp. 322-388.
14. L. B. Silver, C. C. Dublin, and R. S. Lourie, "Does Violence Breed Violence? Contributions from a Study of the Child Abuse Syndrome," *Amer. J. of Psychiatry*, 126 (No. 3, September 1969):407.
15. *Ibid.*
16. B. F. Steele, "Violence in Our Society," *op. cit.*, p. 46.
17. Unpublished study by Dr. J. Weston, School of Medicine, University of Utah, Salt Lake City, Utah.
18. G. M. Duncan, S. H. Frazier, E. M. Litin, A. M. Johnson and

A. J. Barron, "Etiological Factors in First Degree Murder," *J. Amer. Med. Assoc.*, 168 (No. 13, November 1958): 1755-1758.

19. *Minutes of Proceedings and Evidence of the Standing Committee on Health, Welfare and Social Affairs*, Ottawa, Issue No. 31, December 16, 1975, p. 12.

20. James A. McGrath (M.P.), Notes for a Brief to the National Task Force Study on the Status of the Child in Canadian Society: The Child as a Citizen, Toronto, September 17, 1976, pp. 27-29.

21. *The Legal Rights of Children*, published by The Canadian Mental Health Assoc., Quebec Division, 1973.

NOTES TO CHAPTER 14

1. D. N. Daniels, M. F. Gilula, F. M. Ochberg, eds., *Violence and the Struggle for Existence*, Boston: Little, Brown, 1970.
2. E. Merriam, "We Are Teaching Our Children That Violence is Fun," *Ladies Home Journal*, October 1964.
3. L. Swift, *Violence and Television*. A paper prepared for the Edmonton Branch Voice of Women, 1969.
4. H. M. McLuhan, *Understanding Media; The Extensions of Man*, New York: McGraw-Hill, 1964.
5. A. Bandura, D. Ross and S. A. Ross, "Transmission of Aggression Through Imitation of Aggressive Models," *Journal of Abnormal and Social Psychology* 63 (No. 3):575-582.
6. *The Effects of Television on Children and Adolescents*, prepared by The International Association for Mass Communication Research. Editor Wilbur Schramm, 1964, UNESCO, No. 43.
7. R. S. Albert, "The Role of Mass Media and the Effect of Aggressive Film Content Upon Children's Aggressive Responses and Identification Choices," *Genetic Psychology Monographs*, No. 5, 1957, pp. 221-285.
8. R. H. Walters, D. E. Thomas and C. W. Acker, "Enhancement of Punitive Behaviour by Audio-Visual Displays," *Science*, No. 136, 1962, pp. 872-873.
9. A. Montagu, *Man and Aggression*, London: Oxford University Press, 1968.
10. J. H. Pollack, "An Interview With Dr. John Spiegel: What You Can Do to Help Stop Violence," *Family Circle*, October 1968, Vol. 73, #4, p. 79.
11. *Ibid.*
12. *Ibid.*
13. *Ibid.*
14. *Ibid.*
15. Santiago Genoves, *Is Peace Inevitable?*, New York: Walker and Company, 1970, pp. 15-32.
16. G. Gorer, "Man Has No 'Killer' Instinct," in *Man and Aggression*, ed. Ashley Montagu, London, Oxford, New York: Oxford University Press, 1968.

17. Ashley Montagu, "The New Litany of Innate Depravity," in *Man and Aggression.*
18. "Average Americans Tell What Should Be Done to Parents Who Beat Their Children," *National Enquirer*, Vol. 44, No. 48, August 2, 1970.
19. L. Eiseley, *The Immense Journey.* New York: Vintage Books, 1946, p. 140.

NOTES TO CHAPTER 15

1. B. F. Steele and C. B. Pollock, in Helfer and Kempe, *The Battered Child*, p. 104.
2. Children's Bureau, *Infant Care*, publication No. 8. Washington: United States Department of Health, Education and Welfare, 1955.
3. Children's Bureau, *Your Child from One to Six*, publication No. 30. Washington: Social Security Administration, 1945 (Revised).
4. Children's Bureau, *Your Child from Six to Twelve*, publication No. 324. Washington: Social Security Administration.
5. Arnold Gesell and Frances L. Ilg, *Infant and Child in the Culture of Today*, New York: Harper and Bros., 1943.
6. Arnold Gesell and Frances L. Ilg, *The Child from Five to Ten*, New York: Harper and Bros., 1946.
7. H. K. Silver, C. H. Kempe and Ruth S. Kempe, *Healthy Babies, Happy Parents*, New York: McGraw-Hill, 1958 and 1960.
8. A. S. Neill, *Summerhill: A Radical Approach to Child Rearing*, New York: Hart, 1960.
9. A. S. Neill, *Freedom – Not License*, New York: Hart, 1966.
10. B. F. Steele, "Violence in Our Society," *op. cit.*, p. 47.
11. D. G. Gil, *Violence Against Children*, p. 142.
12. *Criminal Code (1955)*, Stat. Can. 1955, S. 43.
13. D. G. Gil, *op. cit.*, p. 144.
14. A. Winter, "Serious Consequences of Minor Head Injuries," *Trauma*, Vol. 5, No. 3, 1963, pp. 3-39.
15. H. N. Krige, "The Abused Child Complex and its Characteristic X-Ray Findings," *S. Afr. Med. J.*, 1966, 40:490-493.
16. M. V. Van Stolk, *Man and Woman.*
17. L. von Bertalonffy, *Robots, Men and Minds: Psychology in the Modern World*, New York: G. Braziller, 1967.

NOTES TO CHAPTER 16

1. H. Arendt, "Reflections on Violence," *New York Review of Books*, 12, No. 4, February 27, 1969.
2. J. M. Cameron, "On Violence," *New York Review of Books*, 15, No. 1, July 2, 1970.

3. J. Henry, *Culture Against Man*, New York: Random House, 1964, pp. 322-388.
4. B. F. Steele and C. B. Pollock, "A Psychiatric Study of Parents Who Abuse Infants and Small Children," in Helfer and Kempe, *The Battered Child*, p. 104.
5. L. Young, *Wednesday's Children*, New York: McGraw-Hill, 1964.
6. G. Gorer, "Man Has No 'Killer' Instinct," in Montagu, *Man and Aggression*, p. 34.
7. D. G. Gil, *Violence Against Children*, p. 8
8. G. Gorer, *loc. cit.*
9. J. R. Seeley, "Social Science? Some Probabitive Problems," in *Sociology on Trial*, ed. Maurice Stein and Arthur Vidich, Englewood Cliffs: Prentice-Hall, 1963.
10. Jules Henry, *Culture Against Man*, New York: Random House, 1963, p. 292.
11. S. Milgram, "A Behavioral Study of Obedience," *The Journal of Abnormal and Social Psychology*, 1963, 67:371-378.
12. C. Hampden-Turner, *Radical Man, The Process of Psycho-Social Development*, pp. 98-99.
13. D. G. Gil, *op. cit.*, p. 126.
14. C. Hampden-Turner, *op. cit.*, p. 37.

NOTES TO CHAPTER 17

1. J. Roberts, "Characteristics of the Abused Child and His Family: An Agency Study." Thesis submitted for course in social work, Carleton University, School of Social Work, 1968, p. 82.
2. C. M. Garber, "Eskimo Infanticide," *Scientific Monthly*, Vol. 64, February 1947, p. 99.
3. S. X. Radbill, "A History of Child Abuse and Infanticide," in *The Battered Child*, p. 5.
4. *Ibid.*
5. *Ibid.* For the recent comments of the American Academy of Pediatrics, see "Report of the Ad Hoc Task Force on Circumcision," *Pediatrics*, Vol. 56, No. 4 (October 1975), pp. 610-611.
6. S. N. Kramer, *From the Tablets of Sumer: Twenty-Five Firsts in Man's Recorded History*, Indian Hills, Colorado: Falcon's Wing, 1956.
7. S. X. Radbill, *op. cit.*, p. 3.
8. *Ibid.*
9. E. Elmer, "Abused Young Children Seen in Hospitals," *Social Work*, 5 (No. 4, October 1960): pp. 98-102.
10. E. Godfrey, *English Children in Olden Time*, London: Methuen, 1907.
11. A. M. Earle, *Child Life in Colonial Days*, New York: Macmillan, 1926, pp. 191-210.

12. A. Cumming, "Discipline: An Historical Examination," *Paedagogical Historica*, 1969, 9:366-379.

13. B. Russell, *Education and the Good Life*, New York: Boni and Liveright, 1926.

14. John Dewey, *Intelligence in the Modern World*. New York: Random House, 1939.

15. A. S. Neill, *Summerhill: A Radical Approach to Child Rearing*, New York: Hart, 1960.

16. P. Aires, *Centuries of Childhood. A Social History of Family Life*, New York: Alfred A. Knopf, 1962.

17. S. X. Radbill, "History and Abuse of Children," in *The Battered Child*, p. 6.

18. E. Gibbon, *The Decline and Fall of the Roman Empire*, New York: Peter Fenelon Collier, 1899, pp. 352-353.

19. Bertrand Russell, *History of Western Philosophy*, London: George Allen and Unwin Ltd., 1969, p. 186.

20. K. de Schweinitz, *England's Road to Social Security*. Philadelphia: University of Pennsylvania Press, 1943, p. 22, quoting Statutes of the Realm, 27 Henry VIII, C. 25, 1536.

21. L. G. Houston, *The Prevention of Cruelty to Children*, New York: Philosophical Library, 1956.

22. J. Spargo, *The Bitter Cry of the Children*, New York: Grosset and Dunlap, 1908.

23. *Ibid.*, p. 42.

24. *Criminal Code of Canada*, Section 43.

25. *Quebec Civil Code*, Article 245.

26. V. J. Fontana, *The Maltreated Child. The Maltreatment Syndrome in Children*, Springfield, Illinois: Charles C. Thomas, 1964.

27. A. Allen and A. Morton, *This is Your Child: The Story of the National Society for the Prevention of Cruelty to Children*, London: Routledge and Kegan Paul, Ltd., 1961, p. 16.

28. D. T. Suzuki, Dept. of Zoology, University of British Columbia, "Science, Elitism and the Apocalypse." An unpublished paper, 1970.

29. P. Harrison, *Never Enough – Twenty-Five Years with the Children's Aid Society of Ottawa*, Ottawa: Children's Aid Society, 1968, p. 4.

30. B. Rose, "The Need for a New Look at Illegitimacy," *Journal of Ontario Children's Aid Societies*, 8 (No. 4, November 1965), p. 5. Reprinted from *The Independent Businessman*, Toronto Robco Publications Ltd.

31. E. Flacksner, *A Century of Struggle*, New York: Atheneum, 1968, pp. 8-19.

32. H. J. Nieboer, *Slavery as an Industrial System*, The Hague: 1900, p. 29.

33. David Brion Davis, *The Problem of Slavery in Western Culture*, Ithaca, N.Y.: Cornell U. Press, 1966, p. 31.

NOTES TO EPILOGUE

1. J. Roberts, *op. cit.*, p. 40.
2. R. G. Atkinson, *et al.*, *op. cit.*, p. 13.
3. J. T. Weston, "A Summary of Neglect and Traumatic Cases," in *The Battered Child*, pp. 230-235.
4. *Minutes of Proceedings and Evidence of the Standing Committee on Health, Welfare and Social Affairs*, Ottawa, Issue No. 36, February 6, 1976, pp. 7-11.

NOTES TO APPENDICES

1. *Child Abuse and Neglect*, Report to the House of Commons by the Standing Committee on Health, Welfare and Social Affairs, Ottawa, July 1976.
2. *Ibid.*, pp. 78-83.
3. *Ibid.*, pp. 85-87.
4. *Ibid.*, pp. 89-90.